Sexual
Exploitation
in Schools

To the educators and parents
working to make schools safe and nurturing learning environments,
and to the victims of educator sexual exploitation who are striving to be survivors.

Sexual Exploitation in Schools

How to Spot It and Stop It

Robert J. Shoop

CORWIN PRESS
A Sage Publications Company
Thousand Oaks, California

For information:

Corwin Press
A Sage Publications Company
2455 Teller Road
Thousand Oaks, California 91320
www.corwinpress.com

Sage Publications Ltd.
6 Bonhill Street
London EC2A 4PU
United Kingdom

Sage Publications India Pvt. Ltd.
B-42, Panchsheel Enclave
Post Box 4109
New Delhi 110 017 India

Printed in the United States of America

Library of Congress Cataloging-in-Publication Data
Shoop, Robert J.
Sexual exploitation in schools: How to spot it and stop it/Robert J. Shoop.
    p. cm.
Includes bibliographical references and index.
ISBN 0-7619-3844-3 (cloth)
ISBN 0-7619-3845-1 (pbk.)
    1. Child sexual abuse by teachers—Prevention. 1. Title.
LB2844. 1.C54S56 2004
364.15'36—dc22

                                                    2003017809

This book is printed on acid-free paper.

03   04   05   06   10   9   8   7   6   5   4   3   2   1

Acquisitions Editor:	Robert D. Clouse
Editorial Assistant:	Jingle Vea
Production Editor:	Denise Santoyo
Copy Editor:	Diana Breti
Typesetter:	C&M Digitals (P) Ltd.
Indexer:	Kathy Paparchontis
Cover Designer:	Tracy E. Miller
Graphic Designer:	Lisa Miller

Contents

Preface

When I was a sophomore in high school in the 1960s, all of my friends knew one of the coaches was sleeping with a girl in our class. Regardless of when you went to school, you are probably familiar with a similar situation. However, it has only been since the early 1980s that educator sexual exploitation has been widely discussed. It is even more recently that this behavior has been recognized as a form of sexual abuse. Caroline Hendrie's three-part feature in *Education Week* (Drummond & Hendrie, 1998) was a watershed establishing that educator sexual exploitation of children is not an aberration, but a widespread problem. Other reports followed, focusing on female educators who molest male students, and the phenomenon of school districts allowing suspected or known molesters to leave one district to teach in another.

The message from children who have been exploited is "it happened to me, it damaged me, and it is wrong!" The lesson from parents is "the school should have protected my child, they must take steps to protect other children." Educators who exploit children are calculating predators who charm, deceive, and cultivate the youngsters that are entrusted to them. Although experts agree most victims never come forward, victims and their families are becoming more willing to speak out and take their accusations to court. Organizations that provide information and support for victims and their families are contributing to the increased understanding of educator sexual exploitation. I particularly benefited from the material provided by AdvocateWeb and SESAME.

AdvocateWeb (www.advocateweb.org) offers extensive free resources about sexual exploitation of clients by professionals. SESAME is the acronym for Stop Educator Sexual Abuse Misconduct and Exploitation. SESAME, Inc. (www.sesamenet.org) is a nonprofit organization whose mission is to be a "national voice totally committed to preventing sexual exploitation, abuse, and harassment of students by teachers and school staff."

There are many modes of sexual exploitation. Some perpetrators abuse only one child, others are serial rapists. Some exploit very young children, others have sex with children that are very close in age to adulthood. Some exploiters are married heterosexual males and females, others are gay or lesbian. Some incidents of exploitation go unreported, while others receive national attention. Most allegations are confirmed, although some are fraudulent.

Although the vast majority of educators are competent, capable, caring people, sexual exploitation has found its way inside the schoolhouse gate. If we understand the circumstances that surround sexual exploitation, educators, parents, and students can learn risk management strategies so youngsters are protected while they learn to protect themselves. This book focuses on a two-pronged challenge: (a) how to spot exploitation—how to recognize the early warning signs, and (b) how to stop exploitation—the steps schools can take to prevent sexual exploitation, to intervene and get help for abused children, and to respond promptly and appropriately if exploitation occurs.

PURPOSE OF THIS BOOK

The purpose of this book is to assist educators to develop and implement comprehensive sexual exploitation prevention plans grounded in the principles of training, prevention, early intervention, and appropriate response. A plan for preventing sexual exploitation should be integrated into the school's existing violence prevention programs and risk management plan. By gaining a better understanding of the phenomenon of sexual exploitation, educators will be able to establish practices that will help them identify and address early warning signs, and respond promptly and appropriately.

ACKNOWLEDGMENTS

In writing this book, I benefited from the help of many friends and colleagues. Thanks go to all of them. Susan Scott was very generous with her time and considerable talents in commenting on a draft of this book. Pat Bosco, Deb Patterson, and Sue Sarafini contributed to my understanding of the coaching profession. I would like to thank Leslie Levy for her insights regarding the litigation process. Thanks also to Elisha O'Neal for her research assistance. I would also like to thank Terri Miller for sharing her extensive files on educator sexual abuse. Thanks also to AdvocateWeb and SESAME for their untiring work to assist survivors of educator exploitation and their dissemination of materials relating to abuse.

I would like to thank Robert N. Farrace, Associate Director for Publications, National Association of Secondary School Principals, for permission to adapt material previously published (Shoop, 1999, 2000, 2002; Shoop & Dunklee, 2001, 2002). I would also like to acknowledge and thank Dennis Dunklee, my longtime colleague and collaborator, for his significant contributions to my understanding of risk management. I would also like to thank Robb Clouse, Senior Acquisitions Editor, Corwin Press, for his support during the writing process.

Finally, I want to thank two of the best teachers I know: my wife, Mary, professor at Washburn University; and my daughter, Allison, teacher at Westwood Elementary School. I am grateful and inspired by their love, support, and dedication to teachers and students.

In addition, Corwin Press would like to gratefully acknowledge the contributions of the following reviewers:

Janice Goodall, Principal
H.H. Dow High School
Midland, MI

Rosie O'Brien Vojtek, Principal
Ivy Drive Elementary School
Bristol, CT

Gerry Adams, Principal
Reitz Memorial High School, A Blue Ribbon School of Excellence
Evansville, IN

Charol Shakeshaft, Author, Professor
Foundations, Leadership and Policy Studies, Hofstra University
Managing Director, Interactive, Inc.
Huntington, NY

Bob Farrace, Associate Director for Publications
NASSP
Reston, VA

Donovan R. Walling, Director, Publications and Research
Phi Delta Kappa
Bloomington, IN

About the Author

Robert J. Shoop is Professor of Educational Law and Senior Scholar in the Leadership Studies Program at Kansas State University. Prior to earning his Ph.D. from the University of Michigan, he worked as a teacher, community education director, and administrator, and was the Ohio State Evaluator of Student Rights and Responsibilities. He is the author or coauthor of over 100 journal articles, 14 books, and several monographs and book chapters on various legal issues. He is also the coproducer of a number of video programs on eliminating sexual harassment. His productions have received national and international recognition, including First Place Award 1996, National Council of Family Relations Annual Media Competition; 1996 Gold Award of Merit, Houston Film Festival; and 1995 Golden Camera Award, International Film and Video Festival. Shoop is the 1996 recipient of undergraduate and graduate teaching awards, is a past member of the Board of Directors of the Educational Law Association, and has consulted with national associations, community colleges, universities, government agencies, businesses, and educational organizations throughout the United States. He is a frequent guest on national radio and television talk shows, is sought after as a speaker at national conferences, and is a recognized authority in the areas of educational law, risk management, and sexual harassment and abuse prevention. He has served as an expert witness in over 30 court cases involving sexual harassment and sexual abuse.

Introduction

She could be anyone's little girl. She has curly hair framing a pretty, friendly face that sparkles when she smiles. She doesn't smile much anymore. Last year, when she was in the seventh grade, she was an "A" student and a promising athlete. Today she is homeschooled and does not have much to do with other children. When asked to talk about what happened to her, tears form in the corners of her eyes. "Because of what happened, I can't have a prom. I can't be with my friends." Then she becomes very quiet. Her mother speaks for her. "We trusted the school and the teachers. It never crossed our minds that a teacher would almost destroy our child!" Wendy's tragic experience is not an isolated event. It is one of hundreds of cases each year of students being sexually exploited by educators. Wendy was sexually abused by her music teacher over a period of two years. The abusing teacher is now in jail, the school district is defending itself in a lawsuit, and Wendy's life is changed forever.

POSITION OF TRUST

Educator sexual exploitation must be viewed in the context of the special position of trust held by school employees. Parents place their children in the care of educators not only because they expect academic progress, but because they are confident their child's character, psychology, and development will be positively influenced. With every report of educator sexual exploitation, the education profession loses a degree of credibility.

Educators, like other professionals, are susceptible to corruption. They have a great deal of power, they have access to children, and they frequently are alone with youngsters. In contrast, youngsters by their very nature are vulnerable, naive, and in some cases in need of guidance and care. Child exploiters are clever, calculating criminals who stalk their victims with great care. Their primary camouflage is our unwillingness to see the molester in our midst.

Children are far more endangered by those who have our trust than by the relatively rare stranger kidnapper. Some child abusers and pedophiles defend their actions as an "addiction." They say they cannot help themselves. If true, such individuals remain dangerous, and must be treated accordingly. Therefore, if we cannot eliminate evil, we must (a) protect our children, (b) prepare them to protect themselves, and (c) increase the consequences for the perpetrators.

Sexual exploitation in schools takes many forms. It may be an elementary school teacher molesting a student in the back of a deserted classroom, a bus driver fondling students as they leave the bus, a high school teacher having a long-term sexual relationship with a student, or a coach selecting a new victim from each incoming class.

Schools are almost always safe places and educators are almost always honorable people. Even so, just as school shootings created a demand to improve school safety, the recent widespread publication of incidents of educator sexual exploitation has created a demand for strategies to keep youngsters safe from sexual exploitation.

Sexual exploitation is not a new phenomenon. Almost twenty years ago, Victor Ross and John Marlowe identified most of the problems facing educators today. They had no trouble finding hundreds of incidents of sexual abuse in America's schools. They wrote that "it appears very evident that sexual abuse and violent intimidation of children in school is on the increase" (Ross & Marlowe, 1985, p. xi).

Although much of the "safe school" literature focuses on bullying, shootings, bomb threats, drug abuse, and suicide, school violence includes "any behavior that violates a school's educational mission or climate of respect, or jeopardizes the intent of the school to be free of aggression against persons or property" (Center for the Prevention of School Violence, 2000, p. 1). Sexual exploitation is a form of school violence.

In 1990, the U.S. Advisory Board on Child Abuse and Neglect reported that child abuse had reached the level of a national emergency. The report identified the nation's education system as a critical factor in protecting children from abuse. The report was based on the assumption children were being abused in their homes and educators were in a position to recognize that abuse (U.S. Advisory Board on Child Abuse and Neglect, 1990). It ignored the fact that children are also being abused in schools by the very people that are supposed to protect them. In 1998, the U.S. Department of Education published *Early Warning, Timely Answer: A Guide to Safe Schools* (Dwyer, Osher, & Warger, 1998). According to this report, "our best plan starts with prevention and awareness. . . . We must avoid fragmentation in implementing programs. . . . The concepts of preventing and responding to violence must be integrated into effective school reform, including socially and academically supportive instruction" (p. 5). Sexual exploitation must be addressed in every comprehensive prevention program.

DEFINITION OF TERMS

Throughout this book, "sexual harassment," "sexual abuse," and "child molestation" are discussed. Sexual harassment refers to noncriminal but offensive conduct, such as comments about a student's physical characteristics, sexually suggestive or offensive remarks, propositions of physical intimacy, and other behavior that is unwelcome, is sexual in nature, and interferes with the youngster's ability to benefit from school. Sexual abuse is criminal sexual conduct that involves physical contact between the abuser and victim, and a significant age difference between the parties. Sexual molestation is the crime of sexual acts with children under the age of 18. I will use the term "sexual exploitation" to signify the full range of inappropriate activity between school employees and students.

MODALITIES OF EXPLOITATION

Intimate Exploitation

Any sexual activity between an educator and a student is exploitative. Exploitation is either *intimate* or *coercive* (see Figure 1). The modus operandi of the *intimate exploiter* involves leading the youngster to believe the educator has a genuine desire for a mutually committed intimate relationship. The immature youngster is often mesmerized by the belief that a charming, smart, sophisticated, attractive adult is interested in him or her. In most cases the relationship is based on the adult's desire to use the relationship for his or her own sexual gratification. Although in the great majority of these relationships the interest is not genuine, there are cases in which the educator professes "true love." Regardless of the sincerity of the adult's motivation, the intent is irrelevant; the impact of the behavior is exploitative.

Two of the best known "true love" *intimate exploiters* are women. Mary Kay Letourneau was a 34-year-old mother of four. Vili Fualaau was a precocious 12-year-old in her class. Letourneau became pregnant with the couple's daughter, Audrey. Their second child, Alexis, was conceived after Letourneau had pleaded guilty to child rape and received a seven-and-a-half-year prison term. Both Fualaau and Letourneau characterized their relationship as one of love, and even wrote a book together—*Un Seul Crime, L'Amour*, or *Only One Crime, Love* (Johnson, 2002).

Another case of "true love" exploitation involved a California teacher. Twenty-three-year-old high school science teacher Tanya Hadden wrote 15-year-old Richard Peña notes professing her love. Peña said that on his first trip to Las Vegas she took him to casino-hotels for three days of sex. Hadden was charged with first-degree kidnapping, eight counts of statutory sexual seduction, and eight counts of sex between a teacher or school employee and a student. The police reported that during their conversations with Hadden she was overly concerned with Peña's well-being, wanting to make sure he was fed and taken care of (Puit, 2002, p. 1B).

Regardless of the way the exploiter describes the relationship, after it ends most youngsters view it quite differently. When asked if she would use the term "love" to describe how she felt about the teacher who eventually raped her, Kristin said,

> I know I never said those words to him . . . I was so confused . . . I really did not know what love was . . . perhaps for a short time I may have thought I was in love . . . but that was quite distorted because he kept telling me this was love . . . all of the definitions were coming from him. . . . He told me he never knew a woman as sensitive as me . . . . He told me he was going to divorce his wife and marry me . . . he told me that what we were doing was what people who were in love did. . . . He kept doing things to me that I had never done . . . I was always scared and never knew what was coming next. . . . He made me do things that I knew I should not do, but I did not know how to stop. . . . I truly hate the fact that he was my first kiss, touch, etc. . . . Now I am confused about what love really is. . . . It makes me very sad when I hear people speak of their "firsts" because they are usually talking about somebody they chose to be with . . . not someone who forced himself on an innocent child.

An example of an *intimate* modus operandi that was overtly manipulative was described by a Boston Assistant District Attorney who urged a judge to send serial child molester Christopher Reardon to prison for 50 to 75 years. "This man is nothing less than a predatory pedophile. He is a child molester. . . . This defendant focused his life, everything he did, on accessing children" (Farmer, 2001, p. A1). The defendant pleaded guilty to 75 of 129 criminal counts relating to a five-year sexual assault on nearly three dozen prepubescent boys. The Assistant District Attorney said "the defendant never did any good for any child unless it would eventually get him some sort of sexual gratification" (p. A1).

Whether the relationship is based on "true love" or manipulation, the *intimate exploiter* knows how his or her victims are vulnerable and uses this knowledge, gained through his or her professional relationship with the youngsters, to manipulate them. It is at this point that the victim "consents" to the sexual relationship. (For a detailed discussion of consent, see Chapter 2.) There is only "consent" in the sense that the child is not threatened or physically forced to engage in the sexual acts. In the "true love" form of molestation, the abuse usually continues until the exploitation is discovered. However, in the manipulative form of molestation the child is usually discarded after the molester tires of him or her and moves on to another victim. The "true love" molester generally has only one victim, whereas the manipulative molester usually has a series of victims, sometimes

Figure 1 Modalities of Exploitation

Modalities of Exploitation

Category	Intimate	
	True Love	**Manipulative**
Similarities	Both involve leading the youngster to believe the educator has a genuine desire for a mutually committed intimate relationship.	
Differences	1. Educator is in love with the youngster. 2. Educator has a sexual relationship with only one student. 3. Relationship exposed or discovered by others. 4. Relationship often continues after discovery.	1. Educator using relationship for own sexual gratification. 2. Educator has multiple sequential relationships. 3. Relationship exposed by youngster or others. 4. Relationship ends with discovery.

	Coercive	
	Subtle Coercion	**Overt Coercion**
Similarities	Educator pretends to be sincerely interested in well-being of youngster.	
Differences	1. Educator manipulates youngster not to tell anyone. 2. Educator rewards youngster with a benefit or privilege.	1. Educator directly warns youngster not to tell anyone. 2. Educator threatens to withhold something the youngster wants. 3. Educator threatens harm to self, youngster, or others if youngster tells anyone. 4. Educator uses physical force to keep the youngster from telling anyone. 5. Educator retaliates against the youngster if the youngster reports the exploitation.

© 2003 Robert J. Shoop

continuing for decades. The manipulative exploiter continues abusing youngsters until discovered.

Coercive Exploitation

The *coercive exploiter* may or may not pretend to be sincerely interested in the youngster. This molester uses either subtle or overt coercion to achieve the goal of a sexual relationship. He or she either threatens to withhold something the youngster desires, or promises to reward the youngster with a benefit or privilege. In this form of exploitation, the adult is very direct in informing the student that telling anyone will result in very negative consequences. The adult forces the child to continue in the relationship by using fear, intimidation, and sometimes physical force. The following example illustrates the overt coercion modus operandi: A young woman told police her high school coach raped her, punched her in the ribs, and threatened to harm her if she reported the assaults. The teacher "demonstrated a pattern of angry, aggressive and abusive behavior [that] frightened and intimidated [the student], so much so that she was afraid to report his behavior. The teacher would also frequently pull her out of class in order to remind her of his threats" (Schubert, 2002).

Educator sexual exploitation is not a spontaneous act. The adult abuser puts quite a bit of time into planning the seduction. However, parents, other educators, and most important, students don't give much thought to abuse. Consequently, unless students are well-prepared by parents and the school district, they are vulnerable. Child molesters are highly motivated and can easily overpower the resistance of a young child. Consequently, it is critical that parents and educators teach their children how to protect themselves from child molesters. (For a detailed discussion of training for students, see Chapter 9.)

1

Sexual Exploitation

FORMS OF SEXUAL EXPLOITATION

To exploit someone is to make use of him or her for one's own ends by playing on a weakness or vulnerability. Those with power have the inherent potential to exploit those without power. A manipulative educator can exploit a student's respect, innocence, naïveté, need for affection, insecurity, or low self-concept.

When parents send their children to school they trust that the people who work at that school will always act in the child's best interest. Unfortunately, some people take advantage of this trust. Sexual exploitation does not always include sexual contact. It can range from hostile environment sexual harassment to rape. The shroud of secrecy that has surrounded sexual molestation of children is beginning to lift. However, with the increased discussion of the topic has come confusion about who molests children and why they do it. Some confuse pedophilia and child abuse. Some confuse sexual harassment and sexual abuse. Others assume all men who molest boys are homosexuals.

SEXUAL HARASSMENT

Sexual harassment devastates the victim, can destroy the career of the harasser, may seriously damage the reputation of the school district, and is a violation of Title IX of the Education Amendments of 1972.

Title IX prohibits discrimination on the basis of sex in educational programs or activities that receive federal financial assistance. It covers both employees and students and virtually all activities of a school district. Title IX states, "No person in the United States shall, on the basis of sex, be excluded from participation in, be denied the benefits of, or be subjected to discrimination under any educational program or activity receiving Federal financial assistance." It is enforced by the Office for Civil Rights (OCR) of the U.S. Department of Education. Under Title IX, educators and students may sue to collect monetary damages from a school and the school may lose federal funding.

Title IX's prohibition against sexual harassment does not extend to nonsexual touching. There are legitimate reasons for an educator to touch a student. For example, a vocal music teacher showing a student the correct way to breathe, an instrumental music teacher demonstrating the proper way to hold a musical instrument, a basketball coach demonstrating the proper way to block out another player, or an elementary school teacher consoling a child with a skinned knee by putting his arm on the child's shoulder is not sexual harassment. Some school districts are so worried about having an employee charged with sexual harassment that they have overreacted by adopting policies prohibiting school employees from having any physical contact other than a "handshake."

Sexual harassment is unwelcome contact of a sexual nature that interferes with a school employee's ability to do his or her job or with a student's ability to enjoy the benefits of an education. The first two subsections of the U.S. Equal Employment Opportunity Commission (EEOC) guidelines define "quid pro quo" harassment. The third subsection describes "hostile environment" sexual harassment. Incidents of quid pro quo and hostile environment sexual harassment are daily occurrences in our elementary and secondary schools (American Association of University Women [AAUW], 2001).

Just as most parents are not aware their sons and daughters may be sexually harassed in school, the amount of litigation in this area indicates some educators are unaware of the extent of the problem. This does not mean these educators do not see the offensive behavior—they often simply do not recognize it as sexual exploitation. Some educators do not understand their responsibility to ensure that sexual harassment does not take place in their schools. In addition to a violation of criminal law, sex between a school employee and a student is a form of quid pro quo sexual harassment.

Quid Pro Quo

Quid pro quo sexual harassment occurs when sexual demands are made upon a student in exchange for educational participation, advancement, or other benefits, or are made under the threat of punishment. Even one incident of sexual bribery or sexual intimidation is quid pro quo sexual harassment. Because of the age and vulnerability of students, even if the student "consents" to the sexual attention, the school and its employees may be held liable for sexual harassment and possibly face criminal charges. (For a discussion of consent, see Chapter 2.)

In addition to certified and classified staff, anyone with whom the school contracts to provide services for the school is considered to be an employee. Student teachers who are given authority to assign grades may be considered employees.

Hostile Environment

Hostile environment sexual harassment is the type of harassment that occurs most frequently in schools. It generally does not involve a threat or bribe. This type of harassment is less tangible and less discreet than quid pro quo harassment, and it usually continues for a period of time. Unlike quid pro quo harassment, which may consist of a single incident, sexually hostile environments are characterized by multiple, varied, and frequent occurrences of harassment. One inappropriate touch, comment, or joke may be offensive, tacky, and rude. However, in order for it to cross the threshold into sexual harassment, the behavior must be either very severe (e.g., touching the breast, crotch, or buttocks), or be persistent and pervasive (e.g., an educator making sexual comments to or about a student on a regular basis).

The hostile environment theory is based on the assumption that exposing students to psychological, sexual, and physical abuse in school is a form of sexual discrimination. Each student should be able to come to school free from fear and intimidation. Students cannot learn when they do not feel safe. A hostile environment may be created by an employee or another student. It may include unwelcome sexual advances, requests for sexual favors, and other verbal or physical conduct of a sexual nature.

Elements of a Hostile Environment

In order for a behavior to create a hostile educational environment, the harassment must be (a) based on a person's sex, (b) unwelcome to the victim, and (c) sufficiently severe, persistent, or pervasive to limit a student's ability to participate in or benefit from the education program. Typically, sexually hostile environments result in tangible consequences such as failing grades, physical injuries, or emotional and mental stress. However, if a student remains in school it does not necessarily mean sexual harassment has not taken place.

In order for the school district to be liable for hostile environment sexual harassment, it must have known of the harassment and failed to take action. A school is considered to be on notice when a responsible school employee knows about the harassment (*Davis v. Monroe*, 1999).

Liability for Sexual Harassment

Alida Gebser was in the eighth grade when she began to have sexual intercourse with a teacher. This abuse continued until her sophomore year, when a police officer discovered them having sexual intercourse in a car. The school district terminated the teacher's employment and the state revoked his teaching credential. Gebser and her family brought suit against the school district, claiming it should be liable under Title IX. They also argued the Court should follow Title VII's imposition of liability for "constructive knowledge." Constructive knowledge or notice means "if one by exercise of reasonable care would have known a fact, he is deemed to have had constructive knowledge of such fact" (*Black's Law Dictionary*, 1999). The U.S. Supreme Court rejected the constructive knowledge argument and ruled school districts may be held liable under Title IX for sexual harassment of a student by an employee when (a) an official representative of the educational institution who had authority to take constructive steps to stop the harassment actually knew of the harassment, and (b) the educational institution responded with deliberate indifference (*Gebser v. Lago Vista*, 1998).

In 1999, the U.S. Supreme Court ruled school boards can be held liable under Title IX for "deliberate indifference" for student-to-student sexual harassment that is "severe, pervasive, and objectively offensive" (*Davis v. Monroe*, 1999, p. 11). In this case, LaShonda Davis, a fifth-grade student, alleged ongoing verbal and physical sexual harassment at the hands of a male classmate. The male classmate was charged and pleaded guilty to sexual battery. LaShonda's mother reported each incident of harassment to a teacher. One teacher reported the matter to the school's principal. When LaShonda attempted to report the event directly to the principal, a teacher told her, "if the principal wants you, he'll call you." When LaShonda's mother spoke to the principal he asked her "why LaShonda was the only one who was complaining" (p. 4). The U.S. Supreme Court ruled schools may be held liable for student-to-student sexual harassment if (a) the school exercises substantial control of both the harasser and the context in which the known harassment occurs, (b) the school is deliberately indifferent to peer harassment, in that its response is clearly unreasonable under the circumstances, and (c) the harassment is so severe, pervasive, and objectively offensive it deprives the victim of a school's educational benefits.

Office for Civil Rights Guidance

On January 19, 2001, the OCR issued the *Revised Sexual Harassment Guidance: Harassment of Students by School Employees, Other Students, or Third Parties* (U.S. Department of Education, 2001). These guidelines do not deviate significantly from its earlier guidelines (Sexual Harassment

Guidance, 1997). The revised guidelines were issued in response to the *Gebser* and *Davis* cases. The OCR connected the Title IX prohibition against sexual harassment to school safety. The new guidance "continues to provide the principles that a school should use to recognize and effectively respond to sexual harassment of students in its program as a condition of receiving Federal financial assistance."

The OCR stressed that both the *Gebser* and *Davis* cases were brought to court to determine liability standards regarding private actions for monetary damages. The new guidance carefully distinguishes the OCR's handling of a Title IX sexual harassment complaint as an administrative enforcement arm of government from that of a court, where an individual is seeking monetary damages. Consequently, the OCR does not discuss liability, instead stressing the process of notifying a school of a complaint and then working with the school to ensure compliance with Title IX.

Frequency of Sexual Harassment

According to a survey on sexual harassment in schools, 83 percent of girls and 79 percent of boys in grades eight through eleven have been sexually harassed at school. Although sexual harassment takes a toll on all students, the impact on girls is devastating (AAUW, 2001).

The AAUW report and other studies focused national attention on behavior that had been unrecognized, ignored, or tolerated. Sexual harassment is not about flirting, humor, raging hormones, or horseplay. It is about power and the harasser's need to exert it over a victim. Many targets of sexual harassment would rather try to deal with the harassment informally, but many do not have the necessary skills. In the workplace, victims of sexual harassment are just as likely to change jobs as a result of sexual harassment as they are to take formal action. Students usually do not have the option of leaving school. Consequently, they often suffer in silence (Shoop & Hayhow, 1994).

Although in the majority of sexual harassment cases the victim is a female, the AAUW survey indicates significant numbers of boys report being targets as well. Both sexes can be harassers and victims. Same-sex sexual harassment is also a serious problem. In fact, much of the sexual harassment of boys is perpetrated by other boys.

Welcomeness

It is not uncommon for an educator accused of sexual exploitation to argue that because no one "forced" the student to have sexual intercourse, and the student did not complain to the school authorities, the sexual conduct was welcome. This argument fails to recognize the power differential between educators and students and the fact that minors are legally incapable of giving consent.

The OCR's Guidance notes that sexual conduct is considered unwelcome if a student does not request or invite it and regards it as undesirable or offensive. Acquiescence in the conduct, or the failure to complain, does not always mean that the conduct was welcome. The fact that a student may have accepted the conduct does not mean that he or she welcomed it. Also, the fact that a student willingly participated in conduct on one occasion does not prevent him or her from indicating that the same conduct has become unwelcome on a subsequent occasion.

The OCR notes that "if younger children are involved, it may be necessary to determine the degree to which they are able to recognize that certain sexual conduct is conduct to which they can or should reasonably object and the degree to which they can articulate an objection" (U.S. Department of Education, 2001). Accordingly, the OCR considers the age of the student, the nature of the conduct involved, and other relevant factors to determine whether a student had the capacity to welcome sexual conduct. The OCR warns that schools should be particularly concerned about the issue of welcomeness if the harasser is in a position of authority, because students may be encouraged to believe that a teacher has absolute authority over the operation of his or her classroom. The OCR notes that it will never view sexual conduct between an adult school employee and an elementary school student as consensual. In cases involving secondary students, there will be a strong presumption that sexual conduct between an adult school employee and a student is not consensual.

School employees must be careful not to behave in a manner that can be misconstrued as sexual harassment. For example, if an educator is seen frequently meeting alone with a student, eating lunch in the classroom with the student, transporting the student in the teacher's vehicle, or counseling the student on nonacademic issues, this teacher is vulnerable to charges of sexual harassment.

The AAUW study reported that only about five percent of the students who believed they had been sexually harassed reported the harassment. It is not uncommon for elementary school students who are being sexually harassed to tell their parents they are ill and cannot go to school. Other victims of sexual harassment become withdrawn and avoid interaction with their peers (AAUW, 2001).

Severe, Persistent, or Pervasive

Although a single instance of quid pro quo harassment is a violation of Title IX, hostile environment sexual harassment must be severe, persistent, or pervasive enough to limit a student's ability to participate in or benefit from the education program, or create a hostile or abusive educational environment. When attempting to determine whether conduct is sufficiently severe, persistent, or pervasive, the OCR suggests the conduct should be considered from both a subjective and an objective perspective.

From the objective point of view, there is often tangible and obvious evidence of the impact of the harassment. For example, school records may indicate a significant drop in the victim's achievement, attendance, or deportment, and in the most severe cases a victim may develop medical symptoms.

Although medical and psychological symptoms are common, some victims do not have any visible injuries and continue to achieve academic success. This does not mean they have not been sexually harassed. Although sexual harassment is usually targeted toward an individual, there can also be collateral damage. For example, if other students observe teacher-initiated sexual harassment directed at a specific student, they may also suffer fear, intimidation, and humiliation.

Hostile environment sexual harassment may result from either one incident of highly aberrant behavior or a number of lesser behaviors that take place over a period of time. For example, one incident of grabbing a student's breast, crotch, or buttocks, or threats of rape or assault, would constitute a hostile environment as well as be a criminal act. On the other hand, behavior that may not appear to be too serious when taken as an isolated instance may be sexual harassment when it is pervasive or persistent. For example, an educator who refers to female students as "cutie," "honey," or "sweet thing," frequently uses sexually demeaning language when he is referring to female students, and "accidentally" brushes against their hair or bodies, has likely created a hostile environment.

The context of the behavior is also important. For example, if upon learning a student was just accepted into the college of her choice the student and a teacher spontaneously hug, it is not likely to be considered sexual harassment. However, if the same teacher and student are seen hugging while standing in the back of a deserted classroom, a reasonable person would understand the behavior to be inappropriate. Phoning a student at home to check on an assignment is acceptable behavior. On the other hand, calling a student to talk about non-school-related matters is clearly inappropriate.

EXPLOITATION OF FORMER STUDENTS AND NONSTUDENTS

In *Jerry v. Board of Education* (1974), a high school counselor had sexual intercourse with an 18-year-old former student within two months of graduation. Other students learned of the incident. The court viewed time as a material factor in concluding the private association with a former student may support the dismissal of an educator where it directly affects the performance of the educator's professional responsibility, or if, without school officials' contribution, public notoriety impairs the educator's capacity to discharge his responsibilities. In another case, the court upheld the dismissal of a teacher who sexually abused two students who were the daughters of the woman the teacher lived with (*Lyle v. Hancock Place*, 1986).

SEXUAL ASSAULT

Sexual assault is any genital, oral, or anal penetration by a part of the accused's body or by an object, using force or without the victim's consent. It is one of the most frequently committed violent crimes in America. (Sexual assault has generally replaced the term rape.) Some state statutes stratify sexual assault to include acquaintance rape, date rape, statutory rape, child sexual abuse, and incest.

PEDOPHILIA

Psychologists and physicians differentiate between pedophiles and child molesters. Pedophilia is a psychological disorder that involves sexual activity with a prepubescent child (generally aged 13 years or younger). According to the American Psychiatric Association (APA),

> the individual with Pedophilia must be age 16 years or older and at least 5 years older than the child. . . . [S]ome individuals prefer males, others females, and some are aroused by both males and females. Those attracted to females usually prefer 8- to 10-year-olds, whereas those attracted to males usually prefer slightly older children. Pedophilia involving female victims is reported more often than Pedophilia involving male victims. (DSM-IV, 1994, p. 527)

Some pedophiles are sexually attracted only to children (Exclusive Type), whereas others are sometimes attracted to adults (Nonexclusive Type). In order for individuals to meet the diagnostic criteria for pedophilia, they must have "recurrent, intense, sexually arousing fantasies, sexual urges, or behaviors involving sexual activity with a prepubescent child or children" (DSM-IV, 1994, p. 528). Although some pedophiles limit their activity to undressing the child and looking, exposing themselves, masturbating in the presence of the child, or gentle touching and fondling of the child, others perform fellatio or cunnilingus on the child or penetrate the child's vagina, mouth, or anus with their fingers, foreign objects, or penis and use varying degrees of force to do so.

Although pedophiles sometimes use threats to prevent disclosure, they more often develop very complicated techniques of grooming and cultivating the child by gaining the child's trust and affection. According to the APA, this disorder generally begins in adolescence. However, some individuals report they did not become aroused by children until middle age. Pedophilia is usually chronic.

Some pedophiles keep their desires a secret. It is believed many pedophiles never come to the attention of law enforcement because they are content to fantasize about children. Some pedophiles limit their activities to their own children, whereas others gain access to children by becoming employed in schools, camps, churches, or other places where they can gain unsupervised access to children. There is also a condition known as ephebophilia, which refers to an inordinately strong attraction to older teenagers.

Causes of Pedophilia

Although sexual abuse during childhood is not the cause of pedophilia, it is a risk factor. The majority of youngsters who are sexually abused do not become pedophiles. However, research indicates a significant percentage of adults with pedophilia were sexually abused as children. Most psychologists do not believe people choose to be pedophiles. Possible causes of pedophilia include such factors as chromosomes, hormones, brain chemistry, and brain injuries. Although it is generally believed pedophiles can be treated, most believe they cannot be cured.

CHILD MOLESTATION

Child molestation is the crime of sexual acts with children under the age of 18, including touching of private parts, exposure of genitalia, taking of pornographic pictures, rape, and inducement to sexual acts with the molester or with other children. Although child molesters may be pedophiles, some adults who molest children are not pedophiles.

Whereas pedophilia is a medical condition, child molestation, regardless of the motivation, is a criminal act. The potential consequences upon conviction include

- Being imprisoned
- Being required to register as a sex offender
- Losing the right to vote
- Losing the right to possess deadly weapons
- Being placed on probation or parole
- Being required to be tested for HIV
- Being prohibited from being alone with minors
- Being ordered to undergo rehabilitation

Although child molesters may be male or female, 95 percent of child molesters are male. Child molesters are categorized as either situational or preferential. The situational child molester does not possess a genuine sexual preference for children. The situational molester may not have access to an adult partner, or may molest a child without premeditation. This person is going to molest someone, and the child is molested because the molester has access to the child.

Preferential child molesters prefer children, and usually maintain this desire throughout their lives. They may molest hundreds of children before being discovered and stopped. In prison interviews, they often state that if released, they will do it again. Preferential child molesters are very clever and develop a very sophisticated form of seduction. They often become close to the child's family, buy the child expensive gifts, and appeal to the child's emotional weakness. The preferential child molester is a pedophile who has carried his fantasies into reality.

Characteristics of Child Molesters

No single trait identifies a child molester, and any attempt at characterization runs the risk of creating or reinforcing stereotypes. Child molesters come from all races, all income levels, all religions, and both genders. They may be married or single. They may be heterosexual or homosexual. The only trait child molesters seem to have in common is they display an unusual interest in children. Typically they have no, or few, adult friends. They usually find legitimate methods to gain access to children—as teachers, bus drivers, camp counselors, photographers, or coaches.

Stereotypes About Child Molesters

Lesbians and gay men have sometimes been portrayed as a threat to children. Antigay activists routinely label gay people as child molesters. This unfortunate joining of child molestation with homosexuality illustrates a misconception about the nature of sexual abuse—that men who abuse boys are homosexual and sexual abuse is driven by lust. In fact, most known sex offenders, even if they engage in same-sex acts, are heterosexual. Many sexual abusers are married or are in adult sexual relationships.

Same-Sex Abuse

Sexual abuse of male children by adult men is sometimes referred to as "homosexual molestation." The adjective "homosexual" (or "heterosexual" when a man abuses a female child) refers to the victim's gender in relation to that of the perpetrator. It is more accurate to refer to men's sexual abuse of boys as male-male molestation, and men's abuse of girls as male-female molestation. Just as we would not refer to a man who molested a female child as a "heterosexual molester," we should avoid labeling a man who molests a male child a "homosexual molester." Homosexuality and heterosexuality are terms that designate the gender of the person we are attracted to, not their age.

You Be the Judge: Chapter 1 Scenario

Three high school students tell the principal that one of their teachers makes them feel uncomfortable in class. They allege that he brushes against their bodies, touches their hair, and stares at their breasts during class. The principal asks the teacher if the allegations are true. The teacher denies the allegations. The principal tells the teacher that he should "watch his step." Several months later, one of the three students files a sexual assault charge against the teacher and files a sexual harassment claim against the school district. During this time, the district had not distributed an official grievance procedure for lodging sexual harassment complaints or a formal anti-harassment policy, as required by federal regulations.

1. Could a similar scenario take place in your school district?

2. Did sexual exploitation occur in this scenario? Why or why not?

3. Do you need more information to answer the above questions? If so, what other information do you need?

4. Who, if anyone, would likely be liable?

5. What could have been done to prevent this incident?

2

Environmental Context of Sexual Exploitation

When people think of sexual violence, they generally think of a man raping a woman. However, both males and females can be the perpetrators and the victims of sexual violence. Sexual harassment and sexual abuse are subsets of sexual exploitation. Although some forms of sexual harassment may not cross the threshold into sexual abuse, all sexual abuse is a form of sexual harassment. (See Chapter 1 for a discussion of sexual harassment.) One of the reasons some people fail to recognize the early signs of sexual abuse is they do not understand that harm is caused even if there is not sexual intercourse. Even some juries have difficulty recognizing behavior as abusive unless there is actual intercourse. They fail to understand that people who sexually abuse children spend a great deal of time grooming and cultivating the child. When a sexual exploitation case is brought to trial and no sexual intercourse is involved, there is a high probability the abuser was discovered prior to accomplishing rape.

Although most educators who enjoy great popularity or stellar reputations do not molest students, the majority of educator exploiters are highly respected by their colleagues, supervisors, and parents. Perhaps most important, they often are adored by their students. Educators, parents, and students find it difficult to believe their favorite teacher could molest a youngster. Convicted molesters are often described as "the last person I would have expected to do this." For example, in Winnetka, Illinois, students wore black armbands to protest the suspension of a social studies teacher after he was charged with fondling a 16-year-old girl. In Santa Fe, New Mexico, supporters of a teacher continued to maintain his innocence even after he pleaded no contest to having sex with a 16-year-old student. In Cincinnati, Ohio, students signed petitions and wrote letters supporting a teacher who pleaded guilty to having sex with a 15-year-old student. A judge spared the convicted teacher a prison term after the victim said she feared her peers would take it out on her if he were jailed (Hendrie, 1998).

TRUST AND VULNERABILITY

The essential element of sexual exploitation is betrayal of trust. School boards trust their employees to behave in an ethical and professional manner. Parents trust that their children will be safe at school. And most of all, children trust educators not to hurt them. Consequently, children are taught to trust and obey school employees. The concept of in loco parentis is based on the belief that educators deserve to stand in the place of the parent. The educator, like the police officer, is the person that children are told to go to for help.

Oberman's (2000) themes of abuse are helpful in understanding educator sexual exploitation. The themes are (a) intimidation, (b) acquiescence, (c) adolescent naïveté, (d) silence, and (e) the legacy of child and adolescent sexual abuse.

Intimidation

The imbalance of power between a teacher and a student is profound. Students lack the social status, age, experience, and sexual sophistication of adults. One bizarre case of exploitation involved a fourth grade student who was sexually abused by her principal. The principal told the youngster he was a member of the FBI and was having her home watched. Each time a helicopter flew over the playground he would tell her it contained his friends, who were watching her. He also told her that her house was "bugged" and he would know if she told her parents about him. He allowed students and teachers to observe guns in his office and in his car. He told the student that her family would be harmed if his actions were discovered. Most bizarrely, he would talk into a headset when he was alone with the child, saying such things as "yes, she is with me now . . . no, I think we can trust her not to say anything . . . yes, she knows what will happen to her family if she tells anyone."

It is not difficult to understand why this child did not report the sexual abuse or why she was reluctant to cooperate with the police. This is a case of predatory sex where the victim was chosen because she was powerless to resist.

Intimidation can also take the form of playing upon the child's good nature and guilt. Some molesters threaten to harm themselves if their victim tells. Others promise to ruin the child's reputation if they are reported. They commonly tell the victim that her parents will be very disappointed in her if they find out what she has done. Or the molester will appeal to the child's good nature by claiming that his wife will leave him and his children will be publicly humiliated. This ploy also appears to be effective with some courts.

For example, in the case of an Indiana high school teacher who confessed to having sexual intercourse with a 17-year-old student, the judge decided to treat his conviction for child seduction as a misdemeanor rather than a felony. The judge said the real victims of this crime were the teacher's two young daughters. The judge said if he treated the offense as a felony he would

> be harming two innocent little girls who will lose their father's ability to contribute meaningfully to their future support. . . . Additionally, since these two children were the real victims of this crime . . . they will suffer damage from ridicule and perhaps even self-torment throughout their lives by having a felon as a father. (Heline, 2002, p. A1)

The teacher received probation and was ordered to complete a counseling program. The judge stated,

> I have decided the foregoing punishment is sufficient, particularly when you consider the offense involved was one isolated incident involving one person and that the relationship involved was consensual. . . . There is a degree of blame that must be shared by all involved. (Heline, 2002, p. A6)

Blaming the victim is very common, particularly when the youngster is an older student.

Acquiescence

A middle school student's music teacher frequently called her into his office after school. The student wanted to be the first chair in the orchestra, so initially she was pleased by this extra attention. After a few sessions, the teacher began to rub his clothed penis against her back and shoulder while she practiced. He eventually placed his hands under her underwear, put his fingers in her vagina, and placed her hands on his exposed erect penis. She told no one about what was happening. This adolescent girl acquiesced to the sexual abuse rather than resisting. Because she failed to tell anyone about the sexual acts, some people considered her actions consensual (personal communication, n.d.). Regardless of the student's age, this is sexual exploitation. It takes enormous courage for a student to come forward, because at some level she understands she may be blamed for not running away.

Acquiescence is most often seen in cases involving preschool or early elementary school children. For example, a five-and-a-half-year-old boy told his uncle that someone at his school had touched his private parts. The accused claimed the boy wet his pants and he took the boy into the bathroom, dried him off, and gave him a fresh change of clothes (personal communication, n.d.).

The boy's mother claimed that soon after the incident, the child began wetting his bed, talking baby talk, engaging in chronic masturbation, and acting out sexually with his younger brother. Eventually, the child told his mother the teacher often would undress him and fondle his penis. He also said the teacher put his penis into the boy's mouth and rectum and indicated that other children were abused. Eventually, 41 children aged three to six years old made accusations of abuse. In addition to the testimony of the children, prosecutors also pointed to physical evidence of abuse on five of the children, citing vulvitis, vaginitis, a small scar on one girl's hymen, and well-healed anal fissures on some children.

Adolescent Naïveté

Often a sexual relationship between a student and an educator is facilitated by a childhood "crush." It is the actions of the teacher that allow the crush to transform into sexual abuse. Many prosecutors are reluctant to bring cases forward that appear to be based upon mutual desires.

Silence

Victims of sexual exploitation are silent for many reasons. As in cases of incest, some children have no sexual frame of reference and do not realize that what is happening to them is not happening to other students. Some feel guilty, wrongly believing they provoked the teacher's behavior. Abusers perpetuate this misconception by telling the student they are so "turned on they can't control themselves," or that "all men are at the mercy of a beautiful woman," or "you seduced me by displaying your body in those tight sweaters." Another factor that contributes to silence is the fact that some children are taught that sexual matters should not be spoken of. Some children have had no sex education and have no frame of reference for what is happening to them. Even victims who recognize they are being abused are often too ashamed to discuss what happened, especially with their parents.

Ronnie's story helps us understand why children do not tell their parents at the first sign of abuse. The art teacher made Ronnie feel special.

The first time he brushed against me I thought it was an accident. Later, when he massaged my neck I thought it was fatherly. When he reached down my blouse and fondled me I knew it was wrong, but I didn't know what to do, so I didn't do anything. Sometimes he pushed his penis against me. It felt disgusting, but I was afraid of what he might do if I told him to stop. He told me he could not control himself around me. I thought I must have done something to invite it, and felt ashamed. When he locked the classroom door and pushed me against the wall I knew I couldn't stop him from raping me. (personal communication, 1998)

The Legacy of Child Abuse

Oberman (2000) indicates an inherent consequence of child abuse is the problem of revictimization. She believes "survivors of early and exploitative sexual relations are at increased risk for further abuse as they move through adolescence and into adulthood." She reports 44 percent of women who were abused before the age of 18 were revictimized at least once.

SEXUAL EXPLOITATION OF PERSONS WITH DISABILITIES

Individuals with disabilities face increased risk of sexual exploitation as compared with persons without disabilities.

People with mental retardation are often unable to choose to stop abuse due to a lack of understanding of what is happening during abuse, the extreme pressure to acquiesce out of fear, a need of acceptance from the abuser, or having a dependent relationship with the abuser. (Reynolds, 1997)

Experts generally agree that more than 90 percent of people with developmental disabilities will experience sexual abuse at some point in their lives (Sobsey, 1994). Because people with mental retardation may not realize they are being abused, they may never tell anyone.

For example, the parents of a child with Down's syndrome had become despondent because their daughter had no friends in school. They were elated when she told them she had a friend. It was not until six weeks later, when a custodian came upon their daughter performing oral sex on several boys in the locker room, that the parents realized their child was being sexually exploited. The father said, "Even after hours of discussion I do not think our daughter understands what happened to her" (personal communication, 1995).

Valenti-Hein and Schwartz (1995) estimate that only three percent of sexual abuse cases involving people with developmental disabilities are reported. An example of the failure to report the sexual abuse of a special needs student is seen in the case of a Special Olympics coach who pleaded guilty to repeated sexual assaults of a teenage power lifter with a nine-year-old's mental capacity. The judge said, "to take advantage of an individual who nature has not blessed with the ability to defend themselves is reprehensible." The victim said, "It hurt, but I just let it happen because he was the coach. Coach said I can't say anything. It's private" (LeBlanc, 2002).

PREDICTABLE PATTERN OF ABUSE

Regardless of the developmental level of the youngster, sexual exploitation follows the predictable pattern of selection, testing, grooming, sexual intercourse, and finally abandonment. Vulnerability seems to be the primary criterion for selection. People abuse children who they believe will not report them.

Selection

At the selection stage, there are no observable signs of exploitation; the abuser is screening students as possible candidates. He or she is looking for the student who seems to have few friends, seems to lack a positive self-image, has recently suffered the loss of a loved one, or either has difficulty or excels in the teacher's subject matter. Sometimes the student seems to select the teacher by developing a crush. Other than screening potential employees for past convictions of abuse, and making sure everyone understands appropriate boundary issues, not much can be done to intervene at this stage. (See Chapter 7 for a discussion of employment practices.)

Testing

Behaviors that occur at the testing stage are forms of hostile environment sexual harassment. The teacher might brush against the student's hair, buttocks, or breasts; squeeze her shoulder or neck while he leans over to review her work; or give her a prolonged hug as she leaves his classroom. Usually these actions are ambiguous enough that if the student becomes alarmed or reports the behavior, the educator can plausibly argue the action was inadvertent. The later stages of testing include sexual jokes and conversations, erotic photos, or sexual comments.

Testing behaviors are very contextual. For example, a vignette in a training video portrays a teacher talking to a student about the student's lack of academic progress. Listening to their conversation, it is unlikely anyone would notice anything inappropriate: "Katherine, you are having serious problems in this class. Perhaps some extra help is needed. Why don't you stay after class and we will see what the problem is" (Sexual Harassment, 1994).

Isn't this exactly what a dedicated teacher should say to a student? However, the video shows a much different scene. While the teacher leans across the student's back, he caresses her hair as he talks to her. He takes her chin in his hand and turns her face to look at him. His tone of voice, body language, and physical contact speak much louder than his words. No one viewing this video fails to recognize the predatory nature of the teacher's actions. The most unrealistic element of this scenario is that it takes place in front of other students. Most often testing behavior takes place in isolation, with no witnesses.

Although exploited children may be confused about what is happening to them, often other students are aware of these threshold behaviors. For example, when female high school students are asked to write the name of the teacher in their school who is a "letch," the majority of the students identify the same person. This does not imply every educator who sexually harasses students will sexually molest them. However, it does demonstrate that students recognize inappropriate behavior that is often overlooked by school officials. The likelihood that students will report inappropriate behavior is significantly increased if they have been taught what is appropriate and inappropriate, and if there is a user-friendly grievance procedure.

Grooming

Grooming behaviors cross the boundary from questionable to clearly inappropriate behavior. The educator might begin by showing an unusual interest in the private life of the child, asking about her romantic life or her boyfriend. If the student does not reject or report these behaviors, the conversation becomes more sexualized. The educator might share stories about his sex life, or talk about his sexual conquests or sexual preferences. He is trying to determine the student's vulnerability and willingness to engage in inappropriate conversations. The student is led to believe that this is an opportunity to share intimate conversations with a person that she admires and respects. It is understandable that some students are flattered that a teacher is treating them like an adult. Often the student is mesmerized by the actions of this powerful, popular teacher. She does not suspect that his kindness and interest are not sincere.

Most exploiters have a series of victims. These people know a lot about children and especially the vulnerabilities of young girls. By this stage in the devolution of exploitation, the youngster is very likely "in love" with the educator. The educator has isolated the student from his or her friends and family, told her how important she is to him, and convinced her that engaging in sexual intercourse is the best way she can show him how much she loves him. In some cases, the educator professes love and promises that they will be together after her graduation and his divorce. "You are so mature for your age." "You really understand me." "You are so bright and funny, I like being with you."

CONTINUUM OF EXPLOITATION

Sexual exploitation occurs along a continuum. Milder forms, if left uncorrected, often develop into more serious forms (see Figure 2.1).

APPROPRIATE BOUNDARIES

Boundaries are internally or externally imposed limits that define appropriate relationships between individuals. Educators without clear boundaries can easily cross the line from mentor to molester. Boundaries vary depending upon our roles. Many educators do not set clear boundaries between themselves and their students. For example, a conversation with a student about sexually transmitted disease that might be appropriate for a school counselor or school psychologist is likely inappropriate for a classroom teacher.

Ethical educators establish and uphold professional boundaries; molesters consciously decide to cross those boundaries. Without a clear district policy combined with an inservice program, some educators drift across professional boundaries. Students often ask trusted educators personal questions, or ask for personal advice. It is more appropriate to refer these students to their parents or a trained professional than to engage in these conversations. The educator's intent is irrelevant; it is the impact of the behavior that is important.

For example, a well-meaning first year male teacher did not understand boundaries. He often stayed after school to tutor his students. No problem there. However, as his students began to trust him, they began to confide very personal information. A female student told him her boyfriend had been pressuring her to engage in sexual intercourse, and she was considering it. Her parents had never talked to her about sex, and she was afraid. The teacher proceeded to conduct a detailed "Masters and Johnson" lecture covering everything he knew about sex. He even shared some of his personal sexual experiences with her (personal communication, 2000).

If this teacher was accused of sexual exploitation, he would argue that his well-meaning behavior was misconstrued. Regardless of his good intentions, unless he was specially trained and specifically assigned these duties, this teacher's conversations would certainly be considered unprofessional at least. Additionally, engaging in this type of intimate conversation may be misconstrued by the student, potentially leading to the development of an

Figure 2.1 Sexual Exploitation Continuum

Sexual Exploitation Continuum

Environmental Visual	Environmental Written	Environmental Verbal	Environmental Physical	Quid Pro Quo Verbal	Quid Pro Quo Physical
Staring	Improper e-mail	Improper innuendos	Standing "too close"	Pressure for dates	Physical assault
Ogling	Improper phone calls	Improper language	Brushing against	Pressure for sex	Rape
	Improper notes	Requests for dates	Touching	Implied threats of retaliation	Coerced sex
	Improper letters	Lewd comments	Patting	Overt threats of retaliation	"Consensual" sex
	Improper photos	Improper jokes	Grabbing		
	Improper literature	Questions about personal life	Pinching		
		Comments about body	Caressing		
		Spreading improper rumors	Kissing		
		Discussing sexual experiences	Touching hair		
			Fondling		
			Stalking		

27

unprofessional relationship. Without vigilance, educators with a special ability to connect with students may exploit a student's dependency and trust to meet the teacher's own need to feel important or cared for.

Boundary violations compromise the integrity and effectiveness of the student-educator relationship and have the potential to exploit the dependency of a student in a number of ways (Peterson, 1992). The continued dependency fostered by a boundary violation tends to inhibit the student's ability to develop as an independent young adult. Additionally, there is a strong potential for personal harm to the student, especially if there is a history of poor self-esteem, dependency, or victimization. Although some teenagers are able to escape exploitative relationships, it is not uncommon for teenagers involved in a sexual relationship with an educator to experience very powerful emotions, leading them to believe they are in love and have no control over what is happening to them.

Boundaries Must Be Clearly Defined

Professional relationships demand that educators and students understand appropriate physical and psychological boundaries. Without clearly defined boundaries, both students and school employees may be confused about when a line is being crossed.

Anti-Fraternization Policies

Many educators and students develop close friendships. In order to protect both school employees and students from becoming involved in inappropriate relationships, some school districts implement policies limiting fraternization between staff members and students. Fraternization includes acts of sexual intimacy, or other physical touching of a romantic or sexual nature, or public displays of affection between students and staff members of the same or opposite sex on or off campus, during or after the school day. Generally these policies limit fraternization with students except in school-related activities. (See Appendix B for an example of an anti-fraternization policy.)

CONSENT

In order to have authentic consent, each participant must have equal power. Both parties must act voluntarily and know the nature of the act involved. An act is not consensual if the victim

- Verbally or otherwise indicates refusal
- Is overcome by force
- Is unconscious or physically powerless

- Is incapable of giving consent because of mental deficiency or disease or because of the effect of any alcoholic liquor, narcotic drug, or other substance, which condition was known by the offender or was reasonably apparent to the offender
- Was legally not capable of giving consent because of his or her age

Consent should not be inferred from silence or passivity alone.

It Is Not an Affair

The seriousness of older students being sexually exploited by trusted professionals is not fully grasped by some educators and reporters. The language used to describe these relationships often trivializes the seriousness of the abuse. This trivialization can be seen when news articles describe sexual exploitation of students by using euphemisms such as "the teacher has some boundary problems," "the teacher behaved unprofessionally," "the teacher used poor judgment," "the teacher behaved inappropriately," "the teacher and the student were dating," "they were having a romantic relationship," or "the teacher and the student had an affair." Because the educator-student relationship is professional in nature, all of the above designations are inaccurate and inappropriate. An affair is a term used to describe a sexual liaison between peers, or equals. In addition, the use of the word "affair" focuses attention on the sexual nature of the behavior rather than the professional violation. It also implies that the student has an equal responsibility for the behavior. The reason U.S. states have "age of consent" laws is because a minor child does not have the capacity to make the decision to engage in a sexual relationship with an adult. One of the factors that influence whether a state is perceived to need laws targeting sexual misconduct by educators is its age of consent law—the age at which young people can legally consent to sex with adults. Thirty-two states set that age at 16, Colorado makes it 15, a half-dozen states set it at 17, and 11 states set the age of consent at 18. In part to help protect students above the age of consent, 27 states either make it a crime for educators to abuse their positions of trust or authority by having sex with students, or increase criminal penalties in those cases (Hendrie, 2003).

SEXUAL EXPLOITATION IN SPORTS

Sexual exploitation in sports is not substantially different from sexual exploitation by an educator. However, because of the unique relationship between athletes and coaches, some additional issues need to be addressed.

Millions of children in the United States participate in school or community-based sports programs. Some of the many benefits to these children are learning responsibility, increased self-confidence, positive self-image, learning teamwork, and learning good sportsmanship. Although generally a positive experience, some young athletes risk being sexually abused by their coaches. Reports of coaches being charged with abuse, exploitation, and rape are becoming more and more common.

When parents enroll their child in athletic programs, they expect their child will be respected and the coach will be a positive influence on their child. In most cases this is true; however, it is no longer prudent to make this assumption without taking some steps to ensure the safety and well-being of the child. Many schools and most recreation programs are having a difficult time finding people willing to coach. Consequently, most states have exceptions in their teaching certification programs that allow schools to employ non-educators as coaches. In most cases these people have had no training in professional ethics or child development.

A small percentage of coaches go into coaching because it provides them with access to children for the purpose of exploiting them. A former coach, now incarcerated, reports, "the easiest way to get a teaching job is to say you are willing to coach. Initially I was asked to coach sports that I knew nothing about, but I did it because it gave me access to children." This person said the abuse "often happened before games and after games. I made arrangements to pick one boy up before the others and dropped him off last so that I was able to be alone with him." This coach worked hard to gain the trust of parents: "I don't drink, I don't smoke, I don't do drugs and the parents knew this, they thought 'this individual is ok with my child'" (Goldberg & Winn, 2001). Another incarcerated coach said, "I also groomed the parents by letting them see me with their children—how well I treated them—but it was a mask to get them to trust me, so that I would have access to their child" (Goldberg & Winn, 2001).

"The child molester has found a home in the world of youth sports, where as a coach he can gain the trust and loyalty of kids—and then prey on them" (Nack & Yaeger, 1999, p. 40). This contention is supported by reports of hundreds of incidents of coaches sexually abusing their players. For example, a Little League coach who is now serving an 84-year sentence reports that he misses sex with his preferred partners—his players. He pleaded guilty to 39 counts of lewd acts with children, four boys and a girl, that occurred while he was a coach. He is described as "articulate, cool and composed" (p. 45). He estimates that he "has molested a couple of hundred children between the ages of 11 and 14, whom he first met through his work in Little League" (p. 45). He granted an interview to *Sports Illustrated* with the hope that "[he] can say something that will make sense to parents" (p. 46). He feels that he should remain in prison: "I have a predisposition to want to be around, and am sexually aroused by, young boys. I can't be where I have access to boys" (p. 48).

Amazingly, during the time he was molesting these children he was on probation for an earlier molestation offense in a nearby town. None of the parents knew that he had undergone more than five years of treatment in two state mental hospitals for child molesting. At the sentencing hearing, one 13-year-old victim told him, "You made my life a wreck." A father said, "You're worse than a murderer. A thief steals what can be replaced. A murderer kills his victim one time. What you have done to these children is going to last the rest of their lives" (p. 52).

Nack and Yaeger (1999) report that "[a] computer-database search of recent newspaper stories reveals more than 30 cases just in the last 18 months of coaches in the U.S. who have been arrested or convicted of sexually abusing children" (p. 40). This is "despite the fact that child sex-abuse victims, for reasons ranging from shame and embarrassment to love or fear of their molesters, rarely report the crime. For every child who reports being molested at least 10 more keep their secrets unrevealed" (p. 41).

Nack and Yaeger (1999) believe there are "indications that after decades of being ignored, minimized or hidden away, the molestation of players by their coaches is no longer the sporting culture's dirty little secret" (p. 43). They note that Steven Bisbing, a clinical and forensic psychologist who studies sexual abuse of children by authority figures, reports sexual abuse by coaches "occurs with enough regularity across the country, at all levels [of society], that it should be viewed as a public health problem" (p. 43). Although some child molesters are married, most are not. "The majority are white males who have average to high IQs and extremely good verbal and interpersonal skills. . . . The majority also claim they were molested as children (though only a small percentage of victims become molesters)" (p. 51).

Coaches who sexually exploit children seduce them the same way that adult men and women seduce each other. They flirt with them, buy them gifts, show them personal attention, laugh at their jokes, and generally let them know that they are special. As they seduce the child, they evaluate the child's vulnerabilities. The determined molester is cunning and patient and takes whatever time is necessary to break down the child's inhibitions. This process sometimes takes weeks or even months.

Coaches who molest athletes face serious consequences. For example, in a Wisconsin case, a high school football coach faced up to 90 years in prison after being charged with sexually assaulting a child under the age of 16. The child told investigators that the coach coerced her into performing a sex act and threatened to kill her if she told anyone (Chronis, 2002).

Coaches who molest children generally have more than one victim. For example, while investigating a basketball coach who allegedly molested two 13-year-old boys and a 15-year-old girl, detectives encountered two other alleged victims. The two boys said their coach repeatedly touched their genitals through their clothes. One boy told police that the coach kissed him on the lips and that he sometimes touched himself in front of the child. The girl said she was in his car when the coach pulled into a park and pushed his finger inside her genitals. The abuse of the boys allegedly occurred in the coach's car, at his home, and during basketball practice (Gilot, 2002).

Former coaches who are now serving prison sentences report that they had molested 30 to 70 children before they were discovered. Some indicate that they went into coaching because it "gave them opportunities to be around children." Most of these former coaches report that they never threatened the youngsters or coerced them. "I just told them that this was a secret between us guys, no one else needs to know." When asked how he selected his victims, one incarcerated former coach said, "Some boys would just flat out say 'no—don't do that!' I would stop. The others never said to stop, so I continued with them" (Goldberg & Winn, 2001).

Athletes Are Reluctant to Report

By the time an athlete is molested, the youngster often views the molester as a friend and is reluctant to get him or her into trouble. Because the stigma of homosexuality is very strong, boys often do not report their abuse. Some athletes are afraid their parents will be disappointed in them. One victim said, "I didn't want people finding out what was happening. . . . I didn't know what to say. . . . He was my coach! . . . I was embarrassed about it. . . . I'm still embarrassed about it" (Goldberg & Winn, 2001). The molester is most vulnerable to detection when he or she breaks off the relationship. It is then that the child begins to realize that he or she has been used.

The sad truth is that sports provide the perfect opportunity for adults to sexually exploit children. Coaches are placed on a pedestal by parents and children. They work closely with youngsters, often away from other adults. In some cases they travel out of town together, often staying overnight. Parents have assumed that their child will be protected because there are other children around. Clearly this is not a guarantee. Some experts estimate that a molester will molest 120 times before he or she is caught.

School District Liability for Coaches

School district liability for the actions of coaches is the same as it would be for any other school employee. The key is whether the school administration took reasonable precautions in hiring and supervising the coach, and whether it took prompt and appropriate action as soon as allegations came to its attention. For example, the mother of a girl who had sex with a former coach sued her youngster's school district, contending the school should have known the coach had a history of sex with minors. The teacher and former track coach was convicted of one count of first-degree statutory rape, four counts of statutory sexual offense, and five counts of taking indecent liberties with a minor, and is serving a prison sentence of between 36 and 45 years. The lawsuit alleged school officials failed to report the teacher's behavior to authorities "even though they knew or should have known that his actions were criminal" ("Woman Suing School," 2002).

What Can Parents Do to Protect Their Young Athletes?

School administrators must educate parents regarding strategies to protect their children. Parents should be told that they cannot assume that just because the coach is popular, he or she is ethical. Parents must be encouraged to talk with their children. If parents are suspicious they should investigate. School districts should make it clear that parents are welcome to visit before, during, or after practice. Practices should not be closed to parents.

Most children will talk if adults will listen. One coach convicted of child abuse said, "I did not assault children that I thought communicated too well with their parents" (Goldberg & Winn, 2001). Parents should be encouraged to talk with their children about appropriate and inappropriate behavior. Children should be taught what sexual harassment and abuse are. Children should be told to tell their parents if there is any inappropriate touching, serving of alcohol or drugs, or showing pornographic material.

Parents and school districts must make it clear that they are paying attention. They must send the message that they are going to look for molesters, find them, and report them. All coaches should be required to submit to a background check and fingerprinting, and should be asked to read and sign a code of ethical conduct. Most important, the organizing agency should encourage open feedback before and after the season. They should have each participant and each parent complete an anonymous evaluation of the program, specifically seeking information about any inappropriate conduct by players or coaches.

What Should Coaches Do to Protect Themselves?

Athletic programs are faced with a very real dilemma. On the one hand, they need more competent, caring adults who are willing to give their time to the development of youngsters. On the other hand, many coaches are leaving coaching because they fear that they will be falsely accused of some type of inappropriate behavior.

Short of leaving the profession, what can a person do to reduce the likelihood of a false accusation of abuse? It would be naive to believe that there are no false charges. Consequently, coaches must not only behave appropriately, they must behave in a way that cannot be misconstrued. Coaches who meet with athletes behind closed doors create a situation where there are no witnesses to confirm what took place. Unless there is some type of medical or weather emergency, coaches should not drive athletes to or from games or practices. When traveling with a team, the coach should not be alone in a room with an athlete. Coaches should have uniform selections made by a committee that includes parents, in order to guard against the selection of low-cut revealing tops or revealing shorts. The issue of conducting closed practices can be argued from both sides.

On the one hand, many ethical coaches believe that a closed practice prevents overbearing, verbally abusive parents from interfering with the coaching process. On the other hand, having closed practices may expose the coach to allegations of misconduct. If a child alleges that a coach behaved inappropriately, and there are no witnesses to what happened, it may come down to a jury's opinion of what happened.

You Be the Judge: Chapter 2 Scenario

A high school athletic director initiated an employment policy that required all coaches to submit to a background check, fingerprinting, and to read and sign a code of ethical conduct. The athletic director conducted an inservice for all coaches, at which time he discussed sexual exploitation in depth. The athletic director also informed all parents and students of the policy and encouraged any parent or student with questions or complaints to immediately come to him.

After basketball season ended, the girls' basketball coach was arrested for having a sexual relationship with a student athlete. The coach allegedly had "consensual" sex with the 15-year-old female student. The girl told police that she and the teacher realized that their relationship was "dangerous." The age of consent in this state is 16. The parents of the student have filed sexual harassment charges against the athletic director and school district.

1. Could a similar scenario take place in your school district?

2. Did sexual exploitation occur in this scenario? Why or why not?

3. Do you need more information to answer the above questions? If so, what other information do you need?

4. Who, if anyone, would likely be liable?

5. What could have been done to prevent this incident?

3

Consequences of Sexual Exploitation

CONSEQUENCES FOR THE CHILD

The sexual abuse of children by educators results in significant detrimental effects on the physical, psychological, cognitive, and behavioral development of children (National Research Council, 1993). Because some victims show no immediate outward signs, the consequences may appear to be minor. For some it takes years before the impact of the abuse manifests itself, or before the victim tells anyone about the abuse.

Simpson (2002) reports on a case in which a 40-year-old woman "came forward after more than two decades because she has a teenage daughter and doesn't want what happened to her to happen to her daughter." The Superior Court judge found sufficient evidence to bind the teacher over for trial on charges of sodomy and oral copulation with a minor. "The woman testified that the teacher was her first kiss when she was 15. The teacher took her on out-of-state trips, they had sex in his classroom, other areas of the school, motels and at the beach." During the course of the sexual exploitation, the woman estimated she had about 200 sexual encounters with the teacher. The woman said she has "suffered mental anguish since the molestation . . . after the relationship she couldn't approach a high school campus for two years. She never went to college and she rushed into her first marriage."

In most cases, the repercussions of sexual exploitation begin to appear early, and often progress to very serious manifestations including depression, ulcers, colitis, chronic low self-esteem, problems with bonding and forming relationships, developmental delays, migraines, self-abuse, acting-out behaviors, attempted suicide, and in some cases suicide. (For a discussion of repressed memories, see Chapter 4.)

Some of the most common immediate consequences of sexual exploitation are

- Not wanting to go to school
- Not wanting to talk as much in class
- Finding it hard to pay attention in school
- Staying home from school or cutting a class
- Making lower grades
- Finding it hard to study
- Thinking about changing schools
- Doubting they have what it takes to graduate (AAUW, 2001)

Clinical conditions associated with sexual abuse include depression, post-traumatic stress disorder, and conduct disorders. Other long-term negative societal consequences include low academic achievement, drug use, teen pregnancy, juvenile delinquency, and adult criminality.

When visitors to a Web site were asked to describe the cost of being sexually exploited by a helping professional, they said, "I cannot find the words that convey my sorrow, grief, betrayal, anger, etc."; "I lost all hope of recovering from childhood sexual abuse"; "I can honestly say that although sex was a regular part of my experience, 90% of the damage came from the long-term emotional and verbal abuse"; "He has taken my peaceful nights of sleep—I still wake up with nightmares, and in tears"; "It cost me the sense of being capable of protecting myself, of solving problems for myself"; and "I don't know who I can trust anymore, now that I've learned that the people I am "supposed" to trust CANNOT be trusted" (AdvocateWeb, n.d.).

Sexual abuse of children is a complex and pervasive issue with devastating consequences. In addition to the visible physical consequences of sexual abuse, such as unwanted pregnancy, sexually transmitted diseases, and violence, there are also significant psychological and behavioral consequences. Perhaps the most important consequence is the least obvious—these children are deprived of the opportunity to be normal children. Survivors are denied the right to grow gradually into a mature sexuality, and instead are seduced or coerced into sexual encounters before they are emotionally or developmentally ready.

The behavioral consequences of educator abuse of children include self-destructive actions such as self-mutilation, excessive drinking, substance abuse, promiscuity, and attempted suicide. Frawley-O'Dea (2002) estimates that "80% of male and female prostitutes are victims of childhood sexual abuse, and victims of childhood sexual abuse are 2–3 times more likely to attempt suicide—sometimes they die." Childhood sexual abuse is not a short-term crisis—the effects follow children through life. All aspects of a child's life may be impacted, including psychological, physical, behavioral, academic, sexual, and interpersonal (Browne & Finkelhor, 1986).

Psychological Consequences

Childhood sexual abuse may permanently alter the psychological well-being of a child. Latimer (1998) reports that as a result of sexual abuse, children are known to display problems such as "extreme and repetitive nightmares, anxiety, unusually high levels of anger and aggression, feelings of guilt and shame . . . sudden phobias, such as a fear of darkness or water, psychosomatic complaints, including stomach aches, headaches, hypochondriasis, fecal soiling, bed wetting, excessive blinking, general fearfulness and a specific fear of others of the same gender as the abuser, depressive symptoms, long bouts of sadness, social withdrawal, and self-reported social isolation and feelings of stigmatization."

In extreme cases of abuse, children may develop such psychological complications as "significant increase in rates of psychiatric disorders, dissociation, intrusive thoughts . . . fear, depression, loneliness, anger, hostility and guilt, distorted cognition, such as chronic perceptions of danger and confusion, illogical thinking, inaccurate images of the world, shattered assumptions about the world and difficulty determining what is real, decreased effectiveness in comprehending complex roles, and difficulty in thinking through or resolving social problems" (Latimer, 1998).

Physical Consequences

In addition to the obvious physical injuries such as internal injuries, torn or ripped vaginas and rectums, sexually transmitted diseases, and unwanted pregnancies, sexual abuse can also result in "serious sleep disturbances and bouts of dizziness when awake, other stress-related symptoms, such as gastrointestinal problems, migraine headaches, difficulty breathing, hypertension, aches, pains and rashes which defy diagnosis and/or treatment, and poor overall health" (Latimer, 1998).

Behavioral Consequences

Sexually abused children may display developmental delays; clinging behavior; extreme shyness and fear of strangers; troubled socialization with peers (constant fighting or socially undesirable behaviors such as bullying, teasing, or not sharing); poor school adjustment; and disruptive classroom behavior (Latimer, 1998). In some cases, these problems may continue into adulthood and become ingrained patterns of behavior. Many of these self-destructive behaviors originate as coping strategies that help the child deal with what is happening to him or her.

Academic Consequences

If a child is being sexually abused by an educator, the education of that child may be significantly impaired. In some cases it is impaired because the educator gives the child a grade that is not reflective of the child's work or accomplishment. The child's academic performance also suffers because the child often becomes preoccupied with the sexual relationship that he or she is having. The child may also be unable to concentrate or focus on his or her studies.

Sexual Consequences

Some children who are sexually abused experience significant distortions regarding their concept of healthy sexuality. They often develop dysfunctional concepts of appropriate boundaries and become afraid of sexual activity, or at the other extreme, sexually promiscuous. Very early, the child confuses her self-worth with her willingness to engage in sexual activity. Latimer (1998) reports that the major sexual consequences of sexual abuse are "engaging in open or excessive masturbation, excessive sexual curiosity and frequent exposure of the genitals, simulated sexual acts with siblings and friends, inappropriate sexual behavior such as breast or genital grabbing, premature sexual knowledge, sexualized kissing in friendships and with parents, orgasmic disorders and painful intercourse, promiscuity, and dissatisfaction with sex and negative attitudes about sex."

The severity of the effects of sexual abuse are related to the length and intensity of the abuse, and the relationship of the abuser to the victim. On the one hand, some victims of child abuse believe they are responsible for their abuse and they must have deserved it. On the other hand, other victims attempt to cope with their pain by trying to convince themselves that it wasn't so bad, it didn't really hurt them. Other survivors protect themselves from the truth that someone they trusted hurt them by rationalizing the abusive behavior away—"he didn't know what he was doing," or "she didn't mean to hurt me." In some cases survivors repress the memory that the abuse ever took place (Munro, 2000). (For a discussion of repressed memories, see Chapter 4.)

Because survivors' boundaries were not respected, survivors may have difficulty understanding the concept of boundaries, how to maintain them, and how to protect themselves from those who violate their boundaries. "This leaves many survivors vulnerable to further abuse. Consequently, the survivor may find it difficult to trust anyone. Some develop such coping strategies as eating disorders, self-injurious behaviors, inability to enjoy sex, having lots of sex, poor body image, a generalized separation from and disregard for one's body, dissociation, and gender-identity issues" (Munro, 2000).

Victims of abuse are not only harmed by their abusers, but the damage sometimes continues at the hands of the judicial system. For example, in the case of a 13-year-old boy who was sexually abused by his teacher, the judge sentenced the teacher to probation. A significant reason he cited was a lack of evidence that the boy "had been harmed." However, according to the boy's mother and stepfather, their son is "having a problem adjusting. . . . The peer pressure at school has really gotten him down. He doesn't trust anybody, because everybody teases him constantly. It's embarrassing to him. He didn't want anybody to know about it" ("No Harm, No Worry," 2002).

Sexual Exploitation of Males

Holmes and Slap (1998) report that "sexual abuse of boys appears to be common, underreported, under recognized, and under treated" (p. 155). Boys at the highest risk for abuse are less than 13 years old, non-white, of low socioeconomic status, and not living with their fathers. The perpetrators tend to be males who are known by, but usually unrelated to, the victims. The abuse typically occurs outside the home and is often repeated.

Hopper (2002) has also extensively studied the effects of child abuse on males. He has found that the factors that influence the effects of abuse include the age of the child when the abuse happened, who committed the abuse, whether the child told anyone, whether or not violence was involved, and how long the abuse went on.

Some of the long-term effects of sexual abuse of males are related to the development of gender identity. For example, a number of case studies indicate that male survivors of childhood sexual abuse may attempt to "prove" their masculinity by having multiple female sexual partners, sexually victimizing others, and engaging in dangerous or violent behaviors. Other male victims exhibit a confusion over their gender and sexual identities. Hopper (2002) has also identified a "sense of being inadequate as men," and a "sense of lost power, control, and confidence in their manhood." These fears cause some victims to develop "homophobia, an irrational fear or intolerance of homosexuality." Many male survivors feel that they should have been able to stop the assault.

CONSEQUENCES FOR FAMILIES

Upon learning that their child has been sexually exploited by a school employee, parents are bombarded by conflicting emotions. It is common for self-recrimination to be felt simultaneously with outrage. Parents are angry at the molester and the other school employees who did not protect their child, while at the same time they are often overcome with self-doubt and embarrassment. Although the blame is usually misplaced, it is easy to understand why parents blame themselves for their child's abuse. They point fingers at themselves because they sent their children to school and told them to mind their teachers. They trusted the school and believed that the school was a safe place for their child. Parents often experience tremendous feelings of guilt that somehow they put their child in harm's way. They feel that they should have seen the abuse coming, and should have done something to protect their child.

Guilt can turn to frustration when parents have to shepherd their children through court proceedings after learning that the only way to punish the school is with a civil suit that costs tens of thousands of dollars. Elisa Page, whose daughter was molested by her teacher, said,

> It's like having a vampire in your soul. . . . You cannot believe the financial and emotional impact. Then you have to have family therapy. Then you have to get time off from work to be able to take care of court dates. (Santschi, 2002, p. B04)

In seeking to protect children from negative publicity, some family members may discourage parents from reporting the abuse. On the one hand, the parents know that they have to go public to get some kind of satisfaction. However, they know that criminal cases are public and the details of the abuse may come out. Families lose all control of their privacy at that point. On the other hand, no parent wants her child to be the poster child for sexual abuse.

The children who have been sexually exploited also experience conflicting emotions. According to Sarah Page, a child who was sexually exploited by her teacher while she was in the seventh grade, "it's a violation of the trust all of us citizens place in the educational system. But on a personal level, it's a violation of the trust a child puts in an adult." She fears what can happen to victims who don't report. "Kids that try to keep this to themselves—it can kill them," she says. "And that's a terrible loss. I know that in my own experience, I came close to committing suicide" (Santschi, 2002, p. B04).

EVIDENCE OF ABUSE

Educators should inform parents to be alert to the possible sexual exploitation of their children by adults, and to report such incidents promptly to the school and to law enforcement officials. Parents should be encouraged to have honest and open communication with their children, to ensure they have not been—or are not being—subjected to the trauma of sexual abuse. Parents and educators must join in making it clear that children should report any behavior that makes them uncomfortable. However, in cases where youngsters are unable or unwilling to report the abuse, adults must be alert for warning signs.

As with any generalization, not all of the following behaviors necessarily indicate that a child is being sexually abused. Some of the following behaviors may be part of normal development or signs of stress unrelated to abuse. For example, in the past, unusual knowledge and interest in sex beyond a child's developmental level would be a strong sign of sexual abuse. However, today some children are being exposed to very strong sexual content in the home by way of the Internet and cable television. Consequently, advanced knowledge about, or interest in, sexual matters may or may not be a sign of sexual abuse. Generally, if there are a number of different signs, if there is no other explanation for the behavior, if the signs suddenly appear, or if they are very severe or frequent, there should be concern.

Possible Warning Signs

Young children who are being sexually exploited may

- Have pain, itching, bleeding, discharge, or rawness in genital or rectal areas
- Display inappropriate sexual activity or show an unusual interest in sexual matters
- Insert objects into genitals or rectum
- Act out sexual behavior on dolls or stuffed toys
- Exhibit unexplained mood swings, withdrawal, or depression
- Begin bed-wetting, experience nightmares, or have a fear of going to bed
- Exhibit regressive behavior such as baby talk or sudden clinging behavior
- Suddenly exhibit unexplained aggressiveness or rebellion
- Suddenly fear specific things, people, or places

Older youngsters who are being sexually exploited may exhibit additional signs, such as

- Unexplained stomachaches, headaches, and other physical ailments
- Sudden drops in school attendance or grades
- Difficulty doing homework or concentrating

Adolescents who are being sexually exploited may

- Become self-destructive
- Abuse alcohol and/or drugs or develop an eating disorder
- Become promiscuous
- Injure themselves
- Develop serious prolonged depression
- Become distrustful of others

Parents and teachers should know the above warning signs. However, fear or embarrassment may cause a child to deny that anything inappropriate is occurring. If an educator or parent has any suspicions that all is not well, she should contact the principal.

Sometimes Warning Signs Are Overlooked

In the majority of the sexual exploitation cases that go to trial, the perpetrator either confesses or is convicted of the abuse and is sent to prison. Consequently, subsequent civil litigation focuses on allegations that the school district and its employees failed to protect the child from foreseeable danger. Although in some cases school districts acknowledge that they knew of inappropriate behaviors, in other cases school administrators assert that the warnings were never received. In some cases there is evidence that administrators and other school employees were suspicious, but did nothing.

After an educator is arrested, students and other educators sometimes report that it was common knowledge among the other staff members and other students that the confessed molester took female students on trips to amusement parks, gave them gifts of stuffed animals, took them to dinner, wrote them letters, and entertained them at his home. Some students may report noticing behavior that they thought was "weird." Other students may report seeing the teacher kissing students, hearing the teacher talking about sexual topics, and seeing him place his hands on girls' necks, backs, and hair as he walked around his classroom.

Signs of Exploitation

Sometimes colleagues of exploitative educators convince themselves that they were not seeing what they were seeing. Feelings of self-doubt are often supported by strong denials from the accused teacher. The accused educator (whether guilty or innocent) expresses shock, outrage, and even indignation that he or she could be suspected of molesting a child. The suspect will sometimes enlist the support of friends and colleagues who attest to his or her sincerity and good reputation. When school employees suspect that a colleague may be exploiting a student, they must not talk themselves out of their suspicions. If school employees become suspicious, they must report their suspicion to the state child protection office. (See Chapter 4 for a discussion of reporting procedures.) Student behavioral changes that may indicate a problem include

- A sudden and unexpected change in a child's traditional behavior at school
- A fear of a specific educator

- A new awareness of sex-related words or genitals, or drawing pictures with sexual themes
- A desire to transfer from a class, withdraw from an activity, or quit an athletic team
- Making jokes about an educator being a "dirty old man or woman," or "letch"
- Spending time after school or in the evening at a teacher's house
- Driving a school employee's vehicle
- Being frequently excused from classes to go to one teacher's classroom for non-school-related reasons

Including the above lists creates a danger of oversimplifying exploitation, as if a mechanical list of signs will guarantee identification of abuse. Lists are tools that should be used in combination with common sense. By becoming familiar with these signs, school professionals can increase their awareness of the issues surrounding educator sexual abuse. Because school professionals may be the only professionals that regularly have the opportunity to observe students, they are uniquely positioned to identify students who may be exhibiting early warning signs of exploitation.

In the majority of child sex exploitation cases there is no visible physical injury. This is because there may have been be no force involved, the abuse may not include the child's genitals, or penetration may never have been accomplished. The abuse may be oral or consist only of touching (Dwyer & Osher, 2000).

Reason for Hope

Children who tell an adult shortly after they are molested, who receive prompt treatment, and whose perpetrators face swift consequences tend to fare best. However, in cases where victims are not believed; where families are unsupportive, abusive, or chaotic; and where victims carry the secret for years, they tend to do worse. Most children who have been sexually exploited recover with proper support and therapy (Boodman, 2002).

CONSEQUENCES FOR THE ACCUSED

Shakeshaft and Cohan (1995) found that if the school board believed the allegations of teacher exploitation, they responded by trying to get rid of the teacher, formally disciplining the teacher, or informally speaking to the teacher. They found that 38.7 percent of the accused school employees resigned, left the district, or retired; 15 percent were terminated or not rehired; 8.1 percent were suspended and then resumed teaching; and 17.5 percent were spoken to informally.

You Be the Judge: Chapter 3 Scenario

A middle school counselor noticed that one of her assigned students was frequently absent from school. After talking with several of the student's teachers, she learned that the student was not talking as much in class and seemed to lack concentration, and her grades were falling. The counselor met with the student and the student told her that she was thinking about changing schools. When asked if there was any specific problem the student said "no."

Upon returning to her office late one evening, she saw the student driving away from the school parking lot with a teacher. The next day the counselor mentioned to the teacher what she saw. The teacher said he was a friend of the family. The girl was having some personal problems and the student's mother had asked him to speak with her daughter. The counselor later said that the teacher was one of the most popular teachers in the school. She was pleased that this teacher was helping the youngster.

1. Could a similar scenario take place in your school district?

2. Did sexual exploitation occur in this scenario? Why or why not?

3. Do you need more information to answer the above questions? If so, what other information do you need?

4. Who, if anyone, would likely be liable?

5. What could have been done to prevent this incident?

4

Legal Context of Sexual Exploitation

CHILD ABUSE AND NEGLECT PREVENTION AND TREATMENT ACT

Sexual exploitation is not simply immoral and unethical, it is against the law. In 1974, the U.S. federal government enacted the Child Abuse and Neglect Prevention and Treatment Act (CAPTA). Congress hoped to encourage states to establish procedures for the investigation and intervention of reported cases of child abuse. CAPTA provides a minimum definition of child abuse and neglect that states must incorporate in their statutory definitions. The Act defines abuse or neglect as any action or inaction of a parent or a caretaker that results in death, serious physical or emotional harm, sexual abuse, or exploitation. Abuse or neglect also occurs when an act or failure to act presents an imminent risk of serious harm.

The legal definition of sexual abuse generally includes some combination of the following phrases: the employment, use, persuasion, inducement, enticement, or coercion of any child to engage in, or assist any other person to engage in, any sexually explicit conduct or simulation of such conduct for the purpose of producing a visual depiction of such conduct, or the rape, or statutory rape, molestation, prostitution, or other form of sexual exploitation of children, or incest with children.

In order to receive federal funding, states must provide immunity from criminal or civil liability to individuals making good faith reports. Some of these provisions not only cover the initial report, but also provide immunity for any judicial proceedings that arise from the report.

Who Must Report Child Abuse?

Americans generally have no legal duty to aid or protect others. However, this tradition does not extend to the special relationship between an educator and a student. Consequently, educators have the obligation to act to protect students from suspected child abuse. Although any citizen may report suspected child abuse, citizens do not share the educator's legal duty to do so. The law attempts to impel educators to do the right thing by limiting their liability for negative consequences from their actions. Mandatory reporters must report when they have reasonable cause to know or suspect that a child has been subjected to abuse or neglect or when they have observed a child being subjected to circumstances or conditions that would reasonably result in abuse or neglect. These mandatory reporters must report when they are acting in their official or professional capacities and know or suspect that a child under 18 years, or a mentally retarded, developmentally disabled, or physically impaired child under 21 years, has suffered or faces a threat of suffering abuse or neglect.

The following example makes it clear that some educators do not recognize their obligation to report. Richard Doe, one of the most popular teachers that had ever taught in his school district, is now in prison after pleading guilty to having sex with a number of his female fourth grade students. The school argued that it had no knowledge of the teacher's actions. At her deposition, a school counselor was asked if she had ever noticed anything unusual about Richard's interaction with his students. "Well yes I did," she said. "On several occasions, I noticed students sitting on his lap on a sofa at the back of the classroom while the other children were watching a video." When asked what she did upon making these observations she replied, "It made me feel uncomfortable. I went back to my office and read a chapter about child sexual abuse in one of my counseling books." She was then asked if she told anyone about her suspicions. She said, "No." The plaintiffs argued that their counselor failed in her duty to report the abuse.

Penalties for Failing to Report or Filing a False Report

Without a report, it is highly unlikely that any investigation will take place. Consequently, the majority of U.S. states impose penalties, in the form of a fine or imprisonment, on those who knowingly or willfully fail to report child abuse. Most states use the terms knowingly, willfully, intentionally, or purposely. In addition to having a penalty for failing to report, over half the states impose penalties for filing a "malicious" or "knowingly unfounded" report of child abuse or neglect.

Reporting Procedures

Each state's statute requires the report include

- The name of the child
- The names of the parents or other persons responsible for the child's care
- The child's age and the nature and extent of the child's injuries
- Any other information relevant to the investigation

Most states allow other professional agencies, such as law enforcement and the prosecutors' offices, to have access to the report.

Expungement of Records

At the conclusion of an investigation into an allegation of child abuse, states classify the report as "founded," "indicated," or "substantiated"; or as "unfounded," "not indicated," "unconfirmed," or "unsubstantiated." Because some of these records can be accessed by the general public, and because an unsubstantiated or false claim could hinder a person's opportunities for employment, CAPTA requires states to expunge all unsubstantiated records. However, according to the National Clearinghouse on Child Abuse and Neglect (2002), "state child protective services agencies may, however, keep information on unsubstantiated reports in their casework files to assist in future risk and safety assessment."

The development of central registries, and the use of those registries to screen adults for various employment or license eligibility, has raised concern about the rights of those accused of abuse. For example, some states allow or require central registry checks for individuals applying to be child or youth care providers, foster parents, or adoptive parents. The National Clearinghouse on Child Abuse and Neglect (2002) indicates that information from these registries is "being made available to employers in the child care business, schools, or health care industry and agencies that certify foster parents or arrange adoptions." Dissemination of registry information focuses attention on the need to balance the safety of children with the legitimate rights of alleged perpetrators.

PUBLIC NOTIFICATION

The Jacob Wetterling Crimes Against Children and Sexually Violent Offender Registration Act was enacted in 1994. This Act requires all states to establish stringent registration programs for sex offenders, including the identification and lifetime registration of "sexual predators." The Act was named after Jacob Wetterling, an 11-year-old boy who was kidnapped in 1989 and is still missing.

The Act requires states to register individuals convicted of sex crimes against children. The justification for such a law is based on research that indicates

- Sex offenders pose a high risk of re-offending after release from custody
- Protecting the public from sex offenders is a primary government interest
- The privacy interests of persons convicted of sex offenses are less important than the government's interest in public safety
- Release of certain information about sex offenders to public agencies and the general public will assist in protecting the public safety

Megan's Law

Washington State's 1990 Community Protection Act included America's first law authorizing public notification when dangerous sex offenders are released into the community. In 1994, New Jersey was one of the states that had not yet enacted a sex offender notification law. This changed after seven-year-old Megan Kanka's body was found in a park near her home. Megan had been raped and murdered. The man arrested for the crime was Megan's next-door neighbor. It was reported that he had twice been convicted of child molestation, and in one of the previous attacks he had nearly killed one of his victims. No one in Megan's neighborhood had been aware of his past history of violent sexual acts against children. The public and Megan's parents blamed Megan's tragic death on this lack of awareness. It was Megan Kanka's murder that prompted the public demand for broad-based community notification.

In 1996, President Clinton signed Megan's Law, which requires sex offender registration and community notification. It allows the states discretion to establish criteria for disclosure, but compels them to make information on registered sex offenders available to the public. The community notification provision is designed to

- Assist law enforcement in investigations
- Establish legal grounds to hold known offenders
- Deter sex offenders from committing new offenses
- Offer citizens information they can use to protect children from victimization

Because sex offenders pose an ongoing risk of engaging in sex offenses after being released from incarceration, protection of the public is a paramount governmental interest. Persons who have been convicted of a sex offense have a reduced expectation of privacy because of the public's interest in public safety. Registration serves as a means to monitor and track the whereabouts of sex offenders in the community, furthers the governmental interests of public safety, and enhances strategies for crime detection and prevention.

State registration requires that sex offenders provide fingerprints, palm print, photo, driver's license number, vehicle license plate number, vehicle description, criminal history, occupation, employer's address, scars, marks, tattoos, and other identifying information, which may include blood and saliva samples for DNA analysis. Offenders are required to update registration information annually. (For a detailed listing of all state laws, see www.klaaskids.org/pg-legmeg.htm)

People seem fascinated by virtually any information on rapists, child molesters, and other sex offenders. This interest has had some unanticipated consequences: registration laws are being challenged in several states. The plaintiffs in these cases contend the registry exposes them to disgrace, vilification, and double jeopardy, and it invades their rights to privacy. They further argue that the laws are "unconstitutional because they make sex offenders second-class citizens."

Challenges to the Megan's Laws of Connecticut (*Conn. Dep't of Public Safety v. Doe*, 2002) and Alaska (*Otte v. Doe*, 2002) were argued before the U.S. Supreme Court in 2002. Connecticut's Megan's Law, like most similar laws, requires persons convicted of sexual offenses to register with the Department of Public Safety (DPS) upon their release into the community. It also requires DPS to post a sex offender registry containing registrants' names, addresses, photographs, and descriptions on a Web site, and to make the registry available to the public in certain state offices. A convicted sex offender filed an action on behalf of himself and similarly situated sex offenders, claiming that the law violates the Fourteenth Amendment's due process clause. The man who brought the Connecticut suit said that as a result of this law he received five to six phone calls a day, with an anonymous person saying, "We know who you are, and we'll get you." Neighbors stopped talking to him and he was beaten up. On March 5, 2003, the Supreme Court held that mere injury to reputation, even if defamatory, does not constitute the deprivation of a liberty interest (*Conn. Dep't of Public Safety v. Doe*, 2003).

REPORTING TO A CHILD PROTECTION AGENCY

Because of the access that educators have to children, other educators may be the best hope of identifying children who are being exploited. Consequently, reporting laws must be placed in the context of the professional obligation to protect youngsters from foreseeable harm. A failure to report suspected sexual exploitation carries the potential risk of criminal and civil actions, and may lead to a youngster being seriously harmed.

What Constitutes Suspicion?

All states require educators to report if they "have reason to suspect" child abuse. Professionals who work in school settings experience a continuum of decision making that ranges from a hunch to absolute certainty. As the evidence accumulates, they are more likely to report. Most educators will report abuse if they are directly informed of the abuse. However, observation is the most common way of detecting exploitation. Although observant educators are often the only professionals in a position to detect sexual exploitation, sometimes they convince themselves that they are not seeing what they are seeing.

No state requires reporters to be absolutely certain before they file a report. It is sufficient that they have "reason to believe" that a child is subject to abuse or neglect. Because abuse very seldom occurs in front of witnesses, and because the protection of children is the main purpose of reporting laws, reporters are not held to unduly rigorous standards, as long as they act in good faith.

Some Educators Don't Report Suspected Abuse

Explanations given for a failure to report include

- Lack of recognition of the characteristics associated with child abuse
- Lack of awareness of their legal responsibilities
- Fear that the school's reputation or an educator's prestige would be impaired
- Lack of knowledge regarding correct legal procedures for reporting such cases
- Perception that child abuse is a problem for the courts or social welfare agencies
- Lack of sufficient evidence
- Belief that the child or family will be harmed more than helped
- Belief that reporting constitutes an intrusion into the privacy of the family

Fear of retaliation is also one of the most frequent reasons given for not reporting. CAPTA responds to this concern by requiring that states preserve the confidentiality of all child abuse and neglect reports and records. However, it must be remembered that if there is a court hearing, the reports from educators are made public and admitted as evidence even when confidentiality is promised. Consequently, when educators file a report of suspected child abuse they should give their opinions, but stick to the facts and keep the report objective.

Many of these barriers to reporting can be reduced or eliminated by implementing a comprehensive training program for all school employees.

Although training is not a panacea, without training it is less likely that school employees will report abuse.

INVESTIGATION BY THE CHILD PROTECTION AGENCY

Most state child protection agencies are open to receive and screen reports of child abuse 24 hours a day, seven days a week. Law enforcement agencies are also required to receive and investigate reports of child abuse to determine whether the report is valid and to protect the child. Most child protection agencies are required to make a screening decision within a day of receiving the report. However, with cuts in funding this is not always the case. The screening options are to (a) assign the report for assessment, (b) screen out the report, or (c) request additional information. The reports are generally prioritized on the basis of the seriousness of the allegations. The reporters are assumed to be acting in good faith unless there is credible evidence to the contrary. Reports will not be screened out simply because the alleged abuse occurred in the past.

If the child protection agency receives a report of suspected abuse and a law enforcement agency is already investigating the incident, the child protection agency generally will not conduct an investigation. In deciding whether or not to investigate alleged abuse that occurred in the past, the agency usually bases its decision on whether or not it appears likely that the same child or other children are currently being molested, or are likely to be molested.

Generally, the investigation includes the following activities:

- Interviewing the reporter and any witnesses to the alleged abuse
- Interviewing the child, preferably before the suspected perpetrator is interviewed and not in the presence of the suspected perpetrator
- Interviewing the suspected perpetrator
- Interrogating the suspected perpetrator if there are indications that the allegations may be true
- Visiting the scene of the alleged maltreatment, seizing evidence and photographs, and videotaping relevant material
- Obtaining relevant records
- Making and documenting behavioral observations of all persons directly associated with the allegations

After the investigation is completed, a case finding must be made within a statutorily defined time period. This finding is based on the sufficiency of the evidence, the plausibility of statements, the risk to the child, and the long-term welfare of the child. The final decision for any action is based upon the professional judgment of the child protection staff member. The allegation is either unsubstantiated or substantiated. In cases where the allegations against a person are substantiated, a decision is made regarding registering the person in the state's child abuse and neglect registry.

TITLE IX LIABILITY

Although not all sexual exploitation meets the legal definition of sexual abuse, most sexual exploitation is a form of sexual harassment. Sexual harassment has been determined to be a violation of Title IX (*Gebser v. Lago Vista*, 1998). Title IX provides that "no person in the United States shall, on the basis of sex, be excluded from participation in, be denied the benefits of, or be subjected to discrimination under any educational program or activity receiving Federal financial assistance." However, a recipient of federal funds may be liable only for damages arising from its own misconduct (*Davis v. Monroe*, 1999). The scope of Title IX liability is purposely limited in order to eliminate any risk that the funding recipient would be liable in damages for its employees' independent actions, rather than its own official decisions.

For a school district to incur liability under Title IX, it must be deliberately indifferent to known acts of discrimination that occur under its control. The school district cannot be directly liable for its indifference where it lacks the authority to take remedial action. While sexual harassment or sexual abuse may constitute discrimination under Title IX, a school district will be liable only for situations in which it exercises substantial control over both the harasser and the context in which the known harassment occurs (*Franklin v. Gwinnett*, 1992). Specifically, the school district's deliberate indifference must either directly cause the exploitation or make students vulnerable to such exploitation, and the exploitation must take place in a context subject to the school district's control.

NEGLIGENT REFERRAL

At a time when reference checking has taken on more importance than ever before, reference letters pose a dilemma for many school districts. On the one hand, they need enough information from previous employers to be sure that they do not hire incompetent, unethical, or immoral employees. On the other hand, the fear of a defamation suit has made some educators reluctant to make any negative comments about a past employee.

A negligent referral charge can be brought by an injured third party, or by one employer against another, if a foreseeable risk was created by a reference that either omitted or misstated facts about an applicant.

School districts should (a) have a clear policy on employee references, (b) ensure that all references adhere to that policy, (c) have a centralized reference checking office, and (d) keep copies of all references released.

STATUTES OF LIMITATION

Statutes of limitation prescribe limits to the rights of a person to bring a civil suit, or a government to initiate criminal prosecution. Although most states allow for prosecution of capital crimes and noncapital murder at any time, sexual abuse, like most other crimes, is subject to statutory limitation.

Statutory limitation creates tension between society's need to punish child molesters and the need to protect the accused from the prejudice created by the passage of time. The primary objective of these laws is to reduce the probability of errors in conviction. Fairness requires that defendants be provided the opportunity to defend themselves. "These statutes recognize that the reliability of certain kinds of evidence diminishes over time: memories fade, witnesses die or leave the area, and physical evidence becomes more difficult to obtain, identify, or preserve" (Dunn, 2001). Another justification for limitation periods is that litigation becomes more difficult and expensive with the passage of time. Finding and deposing witnesses who have moved to other states and reconstructing events where documents have been discarded contribute to the need for some limitations. However, society's interest in prosecuting a child molester does not diminish simply because of the passage of time (Dunn, 2001). This is especially true because sexual offenders, in general, are more likely than any other class of criminals to repeat their crimes.

RECIDIVISM

Recidivism is a tendency to return to criminal activities and behaviors. The public's fear that released child molesters will molest other children is justified. One research project that looked at 61 previous studies of sexual recidivism using a four- to five-year follow-up period found that 13.4 percent recidivated with a sexual offense (Hanson, 1997). A long-term study of child molesters in Canada found that 42 percent were convicted again of sexual or violent crimes during a 15- to 30-year follow-up period. The highest rate of recidivism (77 percent) was for those with previous sexual offenses who selected boy victims outside the family and who were never married (Hanson, 1996). Among child molesters, those with male victims have been found to have the highest recidivism rates, followed by those with unrelated female victims (Hanson & Bussiere, 1996).

RECOVERED MEMORIES

In addition to posing an immediate threat to the physical well-being of the child, sexual exploitation has a debilitating psychological effect that may last a lifetime. Statutes of limitation limit the ability of victims to redress wrongs unless they recognize the extent of their injuries before a set time period expires. Although many victims of childhood sexual exploitation remember the abusive incidents throughout their entire lives, some victims are so psychologically damaged they repress all memory of what happened to them until many years after the abuse. Repressing the memory allows the victim to escape the psychological turmoil caused by the pain of the abuse. In cases where the victim does not immediately remember the abuse, memories sometimes return as the result of counseling or therapy.

Some survivors who later remember the abuse choose to initiate civil or criminal actions against their abuser and those who they believe failed to protect them from the abuse. Some take legal action to force accountability, others need monetary awards to pay for counseling or therapy, others say they want to demonstrate that child sexual abuse is not acceptable, others want to protect other children from abuse, and still others want to increase awareness of the long-term damage childhood sexual abuse inflicts.

The concept of recovered memory is not without detractors. In 1992, the False Memory Syndrome Foundation was founded by parents whose adult children had accused them of sexual abuse during their childhood, based on recovered memories. This organization challenges the accuracy of claims of recovered repressed memories of abuse. They assert that

> because of the reconstructive nature of memory, some memories may be distorted through influences such as the incorporation of new information. They can result from the influence of external factors, such as the opinion of an authority figure or information repeated in the culture. An individual with an internal desire to please, to get better or to conform can easily be affected by such influences. (False Memory Syndrome Foundation, n.d.)

THE DELAYED DISCOVERY DOCTRINE

Although statutes of limitation protect people from being forced to defend themselves against old allegations, these statutes have sometimes prevented legitimate cases from coming forward (*Tyson v. Tyson*, 1986). Consequently, the doctrine of delayed discovery was developed to assist victims who did not recognize that they were harmed or did not understand that a law was broken. The doctrine was first applied in the case of *Johnson v. Johnson* (1988). In this case, the court classified child sexual abuse cases as Type I or Type II. Type I abuse involves a survivor who was always aware of the abuse, but was unaware of the connection between the abuse and his or her physical or psychological symptoms. Type II abuse involves survivors who repressed all memory of the sexual abuse. The court recognized that "at some point the injured person becomes possessed of sufficient information concerning his injury and its cause thereby putting a reasonable person on inquiry to determine whether actionable conduct is involved. At that point, under the discovery rule, the running of the limitation period commences." The court ruled that the restrictions of the statute "must sometimes be loosened in order to give the substantive law room to develop." Thus the court held that the delayed discovery doctrine applied.

This doctrine holds that "the statute of limitations does not begin to run until the plaintiff has discovered, or in the exercise of reasonable diligence should have discovered, all of the facts which are essential to the cause of action" (*DeRose v. Carswell*, 1987). The delayed discovery doctrine has allowed numerous child sexual abuse suits to come forward that would have previously been barred.

DISCRIMINATORY ENFORCEMENT

Some people argue that the severity of the punishment that a child molester receives depends on his or her sex or sexual orientation. Female molesters appear to receive lesser sentences than male molesters. Recently the furor over this disparity has caused some sentences to be modified. For example, in a New Jersey case a female teacher pleaded guilty to sexually assaulting one of her 13-year-old male students. She was sentenced to five years' probation by a superior court judge, who said that he saw nothing wrong with the relationship and that the boy did not appear to suffer any psychological harm. "Maybe it was a way for him, once this happened, to satisfy his sexual needs," the judge said. "It's just something between two people that clicked beyond the teacher-student relationship. . . . I really don't see the harm that was done and certainly society doesn't need to be worried." The public outrage at these comments led to a judicial review of the handling of the case. An appeals court ordered the teacher to be resentenced to three years in prison. She was also ordered to register as a sex offender after her release from prison ("Teacher Jailed for Sex With Student," 2002).

You Be the Judge: Chapter 4 Scenario

The principal had heard rumors about one of his teachers for several years, but no hard facts ever appeared. No one ever made a formal complaint. This teacher and his wife had taken a group of English students on a school-sponsored trip to Europe each year for the past 10 years. Four days before the group was to leave for Europe, a former student told the principal that when he was a student this teacher had sexually molested him.

The former student is now 25 years old. He said that he remembered the abuse as a result of attending counseling for a substance abuse problem. He said he was telling the principal in order to protect other students. The principal canceled the trip. The teacher was quite upset, resigned, and applied for a teaching position in another state. The principal agreed not to tell anyone about the unsubstantiated allegations unless specifically asked. The teacher was hired in another state and subsequently was arrested for sexual molestation.

1. Could a similar scenario take place in your school district?

2. Did sexual exploitation occur in this scenario? Why or why not?

3. Do you need more information to answer the above questions? If so, what other information do you need?

4. Who, if anyone, would likely be liable?

5. What could have been done to prevent this incident?

5

Standard of Care for a Safe School

I n most cases involving allegations that a school employee has sexually exploited a student, the principal is also named as a defendant. Some cases settle out of court, some are decided in favor of the defendant, and some are decided in favor of the plaintiff. In most cases, the plaintiff attempts to show that the harm would not have occurred if the principal or other school employees had performed their duties according to the standard of care required of the profession.

DUTY TO PROTECT

In Loco Parentis

The doctrine of *in loco parentis* states that when children leave the protection of their parents, the school takes over physical custody and control of the children and effectively takes the place of their parents (*Garcia v. City of N.Y.*, 1996). The U.S. Supreme Court acknowledged there is an "obvious concern on the part of parents, and school authorities acting *in loco parentis*, to protect children—especially in a captive audience—from exposure to sexually explicit, indecent, or lewd speech" (*Bethel Sch. Dist. No. 403 v. Fraser*, 1986). When parents bring civil suits based on allegations of sexual exploitation, they support their argument with one of five theories: *respondeat superior*, constitutional duty to protect, Title IX, Section 1983, or negligence.

Respondeat Superior

The doctrine of *respondeat superior,* the vicarious liability of the employer, is based on the English common law concept that the master was responsible for the negligent acts of his servants. The contemporary justification for this doctrine is that if an employer knows that it may be held liable for the actions of its employees, it is more likely to exercise care in the selection, employment, and supervision of its employees.

An example of *respondeat superior* liability is found in a decision in South Carolina, in which a jury found a Charleston private school and two former administrators liable for a teacher's sexual abuse of male students, and awarded the victim's father $105 million in damages. Although the award is unlikely to be collected in full, it may be the largest for a single victim of sexual misconduct by a school employee. The court found that the principal was negligent for not stopping the abuse in the 1970s and early 1980s. The teacher was sentenced to 20 years in prison in connection with 13 sexual abuse charges. The teacher admitted to having victimized at least 39 boys. In this case, the teacher was allowed to quietly resign after a sexual exploitation complaint. The principal wrote a letter of reference and helped the teacher get another teaching position (Fine, 2000). (For a more detailed discussion of *respondeat superior,* see Chapter 7.)

Constitutional Duty to Protect

Other cases against school districts have been based on the argument that the school has a duty to protect students from sexual exploitation because of a special relationship between the child and the school. Although this argument is frequently put forward, courts generally have not been willing to extend the protection of a "special relationship" to encompass schoolchildren. Even though the state requires a child to attend school, it does not prevent the child from meeting his or her basic human needs. By mandating school attendance, courts have said, the state has not assumed responsibility for the children's entire personal lives; children and their parents retain substantial freedom to act.

DeMitchell (2002) points out that "federal courts fail to understand [that it is the] dynamics of sexual abuse itself that renders some schoolchildren helpless and prevents them from seeking and finding effective assistance." He reasons that "federal courts are wrong to suggest that schoolchildren can protect themselves from assault. The trauma of sexual molestation, especially by a trusted individual, may diminish a child's ability to fend off further abuse."

DeMitchell (2002) asserts, "schoolchildren who are sexually abused by the very people who are entrusted with caring for them while at school are quite like prisoners, 'made captive by the condition of their dependency,' and are shackled by confusion, shame, isolation, and fear." He laments the fact that the "special relationship" duty to protect has not prevailed. He concludes that "it is a poor profession that does not owe a duty of responsibility or care to its clients. If the school assumes the duty of the parent then it can be argued that students must turn to the school for 'reasonable security' from sexual abuse while at school."

Title IX

Another argument is that the anti-discrimination statute, Title IX, imposes a duty on schools to protect children from sexual exploitation. The 1998 U.S. Supreme Court ruling in *Gebser v. Lago Vista* clarified the extent of the Title IX protection. In that case, Frank Waldrop, a teacher at Lago Vista High School, made sexually suggestive remarks to students during after-school book discussion sessions. He began targeting his remarks at Alida Star Gebser, an eighth grader. He visited her home where he kissed and fondled her. The two had sexual intercourse on a number of occasions.

The plaintiffs argued the Department of Education's Sexual Harassment Guidance indicated the district should be held liable in cases where a teacher is "aided in carrying out the sexual harassment of students by his or her position of authority with the institution," irrespective of whether school district officials had any knowledge of the harassment and irrespective of their answer upon becoming aware. They also argued the school district should be liable if the school authorities knew or should have known about the harassment but failed to uncover it and eliminate it. The Court rejected both of these arguments in favor of the much higher test of actual knowledge. The Court held that damages could not be recovered in cases of teacher-student sexual harassment unless an official of the school district who, at a minimum, has authority to institute corrective measures on the district's behalf has actual notice of, and is deliberately indifferent to, the teacher's misconduct.

Consequently, school districts will not be found liable for violating Title IX unless the school officials received actual notice of the abuse and did nothing. Although the Court recognized the "extraordinary harm" a student suffers when subjected to abuse by a teacher, and that the teacher's reprehensible conduct "undermines the basic purpose of the educational system," the Court affirmed that where a school district had no knowledge of the teacher's sexual exploitation, the school district had no opportunity to take corrective action to end or limit the harm (*Gebser v. Lago Vista*, 1998).

Section 1983

Section 1983 of the Civil Action for Deprivation of Rights Act (Section 1983) is one of the most commonly used causes of action to redress violation of federal constitutional rights by government officials. Section 1983 holds "every person" acting under color of state law liable for depriving any other person in the United States of "any rights, privileges, or immunities secured by the Constitution and laws." To recover damages against a government official under Section 1983, a plaintiff must establish that a constitutional right exists, that the defendant violated that right under color of state law, and that the defendant's act is the proximate cause of the plaintiff's injury. The primary barrier to recovery under Section 1983 is the doctrine of qualified immunity.

Qualified or conditional immunity from civil prosecution means individuals are not liable as long as they are clearly acting within the scope of their authority. If they violate someone's rights while acting outside the scope of their authority they may be held personally liable. In the case of school boards, qualified immunity was established by the Supreme Court in *Wood v. Strickland* (1975).The Supreme Court's rationale for using qualified immunity to shield public officials from Section 1983 liability includes (a) the expense of litigation, (b) the diversion of official energy from pressing public issues, and (c) the deterrence of able citizens from acceptance of public office.

In general, school districts do not enjoy either absolute or qualified immunity from civil action. However, school districts cannot be held liable under Section 1983 unless a policy or custom caused the constitutional violation (*Wood v. Strickland*, 1975). A policy is a motion that is passed by the school district's duly constituted board. In sum, plaintiffs can bring a successful action under Section 1983 if they were deprived of a constitutional right by individuals acting under color of state law, and they were deprived of their constitutional rights without the due process of law.

Negligence

People are negligent when they act without due care and attention, or when they fail to act and a person whom they ought to have considered is affected or injured by their actions or their failure to act. When a person complies with the standard of care, he or she will generally not be judged to be at fault or found negligent.

STANDARD OF CARE FOR PRINCIPALS

A standard of care is the degree of skill and knowledge that can reasonably be expected of normal prudent practitioners of the same experience and standing. Education standards of care are not only the concern of professionals and professionals-in-training, but are issues of legal liability. The standard as understood by a judge or jury is likely to be influenced, if not determined, by the professional literature and opinions of recognized experts in the field of educational administration. Increasingly, the standard of care is interpreted as behavior consistent with contemporary literature published by recognized authorities.

Principals make dozens of decisions each day. No principal is able to check the policy manual before each decision. However, each decision will be measured against the relevant policy or generally accepted practice. Consequently, principals must be familiar with all policies that directly impact the operation of their school.

The following examples indicate how a court might evaluate a principal's actions. If a principal frequently observed a student riding in a car with a school employee, and the school district had a policy prohibiting school employees from transporting students in their private vehicles, it would be reasonable to expect the principal to inquire as to the circumstances surrounding this event. Further, a reasonable principal should be concerned if an unusually high number of female students requested to transfer from this teacher's class. And finally, if the school counselor had informed the principal of rumors alleging that this school employee makes female students feel uncomfortable, it would be critical that the principal know the school district's policy on sexual harassment and sexual abuse, and know the procedure for investigating allegations of sexual harassment or abuse.

Although there might be a reasonable explanation for each of the above events, each still warrants closer scrutiny. If in this example no investigation was conducted, and it was subsequently determined that this teacher did, in fact, molest a student, the fact that the principal did not know or enforce district policies would be presented to document the principal's failure to meet the standards of the district and the profession.

Duty to Obey the Law

Ethical concepts become legal principles only when the legislature enacts a specific law or a court publishes a decision. If there is a conflict between a principal's ethics and the law, the principal is bound to comply with the law. For example, in the case of suspected educator child exploitation, the principal may be familiar with her state child abuse reporting law, but be reluctant to report her suspicion because of a fear of damaging a teacher's reputation without "proof" of abuse. The principal's sense of ethics and fairness that tells her that a person is "innocent until proven guilty" may cause her to personally investigate the allegations before reporting. Laws, however, override ethical principles. The principal must report the suspected abuse, even at the risk of harming an innocent educator's reputation.

Sometimes personal loyalty conflicts with legal duty. For example, if a principal learns that a student is considering filing a formal complaint of sexual exploitation against an educator, the principal may be tempted to warn the educator to stop certain behaviors. By notifying the educator of an impending investigation, the principal is interfering with the investigative process. Additionally, such a warning could result in retaliation against the student. In the above examples, the principal's actions would likely be seen as falling below the standard of the profession.

Federal and state statutes, standards of professional organizations, and professional literature are the most common sources to delineate the standard of care. During court testimony it is a common practice for the attorney working for the plaintiff to ask the principal to agree that a certain source is authoritative. For example, the attorney might say, "Principal Doe, do you agree that the National Association of Secondary School Principals (NASSP) is the leading professional organization for secondary school principals?" Once it is established that the principal agrees, the attorney will attempt to point out where the principal's behavior did not conform to the standards presented in various documents from NASSP. It is imperative that all principals stay current with the professional literature.

Duty to Provide a Safe Environment

Principals are responsible for taking reasonable steps to provide for the safety and welfare of students. Society assumes that during the time the student is away from home and involved in school activities the student's interests, welfare, and safety are under the control of competent adults. Professional literature is unanimous in stating school administrators are the most important players in ensuring a positive learning environment. These administrators are responsible for supervision of students and school employees. Additionally, they are responsible for ensuring that all school district policies and state laws are followed.

The district's duty of care can be understood by answering the following questions:

- Was there a reasonably foreseeable risk of harm?
- What action would have been needed to avoid the harm?
- Could the person in question reasonably have been expected to take that action?
- Was the conduct of any person a departure from the standard of care?
- Was there a cause-effect relationship between the negligence and the harm or damage caused?

STANDARD OF CARE FOR SCHOOL EMPLOYEES

Every school employee has a duty to act in the best interest of the child. Victims of exploitation often allege they either told a school employee about the abuse, or a school employee observed the inappropriate behavior. Frequently educators testify that although they recall noticing "something that did not seem right," they did not become "suspicious." It is unlikely that educators will recognize signs of exploitation if they do not agree on appropriate professional boundaries. (For a discussion of boundaries, see Chapter 2.) By becoming educated about proper boundaries, signs of abuse, and the standards of the profession, educators will come to trust their instincts.

School employees who know, suspect, or should have known about sexual exploitation, and do nothing, are all partially responsible for the continued abuse. Administrators, teachers, secretaries, maintenance people, bus drivers, and cafeteria workers who felt uneasy about a teacher's relationship with a boy or girl failed the child if they did not report their suspicions. There must be zero tolerance, not only for abuse, but for the silence of those who were suspicious and did nothing. In their capacity as frontline workers, school employees come into regular contact with students who are being sexually exploited.

Unless educators report suspected sexual exploiters, the police and the courts will not be able to take any action. Children should not be expected to stop the abuse by themselves. It is not enough to teach children to tell someone. It is the responsibility of adults to notice, and to say something when they see sexually inappropriate behaviors ("Facts About Those Abused," n.d.). Risk reduction must expand from focusing on the victims and their actions to focus on the offenders and those who enable exploitation to take place.

Barriers to Recognizing Exploitation

Many educators do not believe that a colleague could sexually exploit a student. They believe that if such abuse happens, it happens in some other community and it is so rare and idiosyncratic that it does not warrant attention. Many believe that educators already know they should not have sexual relationships with students. Consequently, some are insulted when they are required to attend training on this issue. Unfortunately, it is just such attitudes that have created the educational climate that allows sexual abuse to continue.

Sometimes there is no way to know that abuse is taking place. However, in many cases there are signs that go unrecognized. Consequently, educators need to rethink their views about the extent of educator-to-student sexual exploitation. Some educators do not recognize, or act on suspicions of, exploitation because of the following misconceptions.

Misguided Loyalty to Their School's Reputation. For far too long, school districts have allowed school employees suspected of inappropriate behaviors to resign. Some school boards and administrators are so concerned about their district's reputation they just want the problem to go away. Not only does this behavior contribute to the underreporting of educator sexual exploitation of students, it allows molesters to move to other districts and continue to prey on children.

Stereotyping Who Commits Such Heinous Crimes. Educators who sexually exploit students are often highly respected by their colleagues, admired by the community, and adored by their students. These people are often married with children. Even when educators confess or are convicted, some parents of other children refuse to believe that the educator did what he or she was accused of. Some parents have demanded that convicted molesters be placed back in the classroom. Some have signed statements promising not to hold the school liable for any future exploitation.

Fear of Falsely Accusing and Harming an Innocent Person. Educators are fearful of making a mistake that could destroy a colleague's career. Reports of false accusations have caused some school employees to become suspicious of all complaints of sexual exploitation. Perhaps because educators fear false complaints against themselves, they tend to give other school employees the benefit of the doubt.

Fear of Being Sued by the Accused Educator. Some administrators hesitate to begin an investigation because they fear the accused educator will sue the administrator and district for wrongful dismissal or defamation of character. As difficult as it may be to do, all school employees must be committed to err on the side of protecting the child, rather than protecting a colleague's reputation or protecting the school from being sued.

Disbelief That an Educator Could Harm a Student. The vast majority of people who go into education are ethical and honorable people. Unfortunately, few colleges of education teach about educator sexual exploitation. Consequently, most educators are not aware of the extent of the problem. The fact that school districts seldom conduct inservice training on this topic perpetuates the perception that exploitation seldom occurs. This misunderstanding is compounded by the fact that perpetrators, and sometimes the victims, enter into a conspiracy of secrecy that makes it difficult to find out what is happening.

Failure to Understand Their State Reporting Laws. It is clear that everyone in the education profession has a professional duty to protect students and report suspected abuse.

RISK MANAGEMENT

Many school administrators see sexual exploitation as a "people problem" (i.e., it occurs when an employee behaves inappropriately) rather than an organizational problem (i.e., it is more likely to occur when there is no clear systemic program of prevention). The perception that sexual exploitation is only a people problem leads to a reactive rather than a proactive posture (i.e., districts hope it does not happen and take no action until it does). This misunderstanding of the issue has contributed to escalating insurance costs, unfavorable changes in coverage limits, and critical problems in securing liability coverage for school districts.

Of course, there are many examples of educator sexual exploitation that were unlikely to have been detected regardless of what the district may have done. However, in many cases the exploitation was foreseeable and predictable, and therefore could have been prevented by a well-planned risk management program.

Just because an administrator has not received any complaints does not mean that no problems exist. Students do not routinely report sexual exploitation incidents to school authorities. Twenty percent of the victims of both nonphysical and physical harassment tell no one. When victims of sexual harassment tell someone, 61 percent tell a friend, 24 percent tell a parent or family member, and only 19 percent tell a teacher or other school employee. In the case of physical harassment, 67 percent tell a friend, 22 percent tell a parent or family member, and only 20 percent tell a teacher or other school employee (AAUW, 2001).

Including sexual exploitation prevention in the risk management program provides an accountable means to document a district's commitment to the eradication of sexual exploitation. It acts as a testimonial to the fact that the district's standards are reasonable and prudent. Such a program guides the district into a rigorous and continuing examination of its operations to prevent or reduce incidents of sexual abuse and potentially devastating litigation. Typically, the school principal is designated as the person to manage such activities.

You Be the Judge: Chapter 5 Scenario

A student asked to speak to the school's vice-principal about one of her friends. The student told the vice-principal that she thought her friend was having sex with one of her teachers. The vice-principal spoke with the named student. She eventually acknowledged that she was, in fact, having sexual relations with her band teacher. The vice-principal told the principal and the school counselor about the situation. The principal asked the vice-principal to contact the youngster's parents and schedule a meeting. The vice-principal was ill and was absent from school for several days. In the intervening time, the counselor warned the teacher that someone was spreading rumors about him. The teacher called the student and warned her not to repeat what she had told the vice-principal. At the meeting between the parents, the principal, and the youngster, the youngster recanted her story.

1. Could a similar scenario take place in your school district?

2. Did sexual exploitation occur in this scenario? Why or why not?

3. Do you need more information to answer the above questions? If so, what other information do you need?

4. Who, if anyone, would likely be liable?

5. What could have been done to prevent this incident?

6

Pathology of a Sexual Exploiter

WHY WOULD AN ADULT EXPLOIT A CHILD?

Educators who sexually exploit students ignore all of the ethical standards inherent in the education profession. Most educators react with shock and outrage when they learn that one of their colleagues has admitted to or been convicted of exploiting a student. Why do some educators behave so maliciously? Is there something about the job of teaching that encourages outrageous acts? Are there shortcomings in the standards of the profession? Is there an absence of appropriate education, so that educators do not understand what is expected of them? Or are we merely seeing a manifestation of the law of large numbers—put enough educators in enough classrooms and eventually someone will do something unimaginable? There are a number of possible reasons for educator exploitation. Some of the reasons are illness, lapses in judgment, defective character, and arrogance.

Some argue that educators who abuse children are suffering from a psychological abnormality. This explanation is tempting because it allows us to dismiss educator abuse of students as an unforeseeable, unavoidable, unpreventable event. Psychologists and physicians define pedophilia as a psychological disorder that involves sexual activity with a prepubescent child (generally aged 13 years or younger). However, pedophilia only explains a portion of the cases of child abuse.

To refer to educator exploitation of students as a lapse in judgment trivializes the destructiveness of the behavior. Lives are significantly damaged or destroyed as a result of sexual exploitation. Stupidity is too easy an excuse. Most educator-student sexual exploitation extends over a period of time and is often repeated with several youngsters. Most educator sexual abuse of students is not a momentary lapse in judgment.

Are some educators simply out of control? Are some, by reason of personality or temperament, destined to criminal behavior? Teacher education programs and district screening procedures must become more vigilant, taking action when necessary.

A unifying principle behind educator exploitation is an overactive sense of entitlement and a sense of invulnerability. By looking for commonalities between individual abuse cases, and then appraising educator sexual abuse in the broadest possible perspective, it is clear that many exploiters act as if their position of respect and access confers upon them a license to behave as they please without fear of consequences. Many of these people seem proud of the fact that they "don't play by the rules." There are cases where the exploiting educator was seen at parties with the student he was sexually exploiting, allowed the student to drive the educator's car, bought the student expensive gifts, called and wrote the student at her home, met the student in local hotels, paid for birth control pills, traveled to out-of-town and out-of-state locations with the student, and in several cases had sexual intercourse in the school building during the school day.

In these cases, the molesters apparently believed that their positions entitled them to act with impunity. These individuals declined to accept conventional limits on their behavior, essentially insisting on extending their power into other realms as well. By virtue of the job, educators necessarily get to tell students what to do. Some educators, however, fail or refuse to recognize the essential separation between legitimate deference and manipulation and abuse. Exploiters take the legitimate power that an educator needs and deserves and distort it into personal license to act without restraint.

While there is a growing understanding about the serious negative impact sexual exploitation has on the child victim, less is known about why people abuse children. (For a discussion of the impact of exploitation on the child, see Chapter 3.) It is speculated that people abuse children to increase their sense of power and for a sense of pleasure. "Those who abuse can become 'hooked' on using children to achieve sexual arousal. They may seek children to sexually abuse because they have had a long history of sexual attraction to children or because they took advantage of an opportunity to abuse a child in their trust. They may have started sexually abusing because of their own abuse history or because they never learned that sexual abuse is wrong and is a crime" ("Answers to Commonly Asked Questions," n.d.).

After talking with thirty perpetrators, who he believed to be honest, Pryor (1996) concluded that there is a seven-step process to becoming a sexual predator: (1) unclear societal barriers from childhood, (2) buildup of personal problems, (3) change in perpetrator's outlook, (4) procuring the victim, (5) first abusive act evolves into multiple offenses, (6) abuse persists, and (7) the perpetrator is apprehended.

Unclear Societal Barriers From Childhood

According to Pryor (1996), the majority of the men in his study had sexual contact before they were 16, with an acquaintance who was at least five years older. These contacts were described "as either affectionate and caring or physically pleasureful" (p. 32). Most of these men also participated in sexual activities with other children at a young age. Two thirds of these men experienced some form of physical violence as children and adolescents. The men seem to have learned that there is no penalty for ignoring sexual barriers against having sex with children.

Buildup of Personal Problems

Pryor (1996) reports that just before they began to abuse children, these men experienced a sense of boredom, anger, aloneness, depression, and inadequacy. They also reported problems such as a lack of sex, erectile dysfunction, or their partner becoming less attractive. Many of these men believed that their female partners were responsible for many of the problems in their lives, and were not satisfying them sexually. Some reported that they were losing control in their families and in their work.

Change in Perpetrator's Outlook

According to Pryor (1996), most of these men reported that they suddenly became aware that their victim was physically maturing. The majority of these perpetrators also reported that they believed the youngster behaved in a way that invited sexual activity. Some reported they "were unable to separate emotional closeness, or their need for it, from feelings of sexual arousal" (p. 92). Some of Pryor's subjects reported that they observed their victims were neglected by their families.

Procuring the Victim

Pryor (1996) discovered that abusers gained access to their victims by "furtive" and "forthright" advances (p. 124). The furtive advances generally took the form of moving from nonsexual touching such as tickling or a back rub, to gradually beginning to touch the genital area. According to Pryor, many said that because their victims did not show any signs of resistance, they believed their victims enjoyed the contact. The direct approach included forcefully grabbing the victim's genitals. Pryor concluded that regardless of the method used, the youngsters did not understand the perpetrator's intentions. He found that manipulation was the most common method of attaining compliance from the victim.

Abuse Persists

Fifty-seven percent of Pryor's (1996) subjects said they had sexual contact with someone under 16 at least 11 times, and 40 percent reported sex with someone under 16 at least 21 times. Although some had just one victim and never progressed beyond fondling, most progressed from fondling to sexual intercourse. Pryor discovered that although some of these men kept their victims from reporting the abuse by warning them about negative consequences to the victim and his or her family members, many of the perpetrators depended on the victim's shame and guilt to keep them quiet.

Multiple Offenses

Pryor (1996) and others have found that child molesters continue until they are apprehended. Although some molesters reported feeling guilt, others said the molestation made them "feel young again" (p. 161). Usually the molestation was reported by someone other than the victim.

According to Groth (1982), male sexual abusers appear more submissive than assertive, especially in relationships; feel isolated; feel fearful, depressed, and doubtful of their own worth; and do not seem to be able to derive pleasure from or feel security in life. He believes that male sex offenders are either fixated or regressed.

Children become the main sexual interest of the fixated abuser during adolescence. This type of molester has little stability in his life and was likely molested as an adolescent. On the other hand, the regressed offender generally is married and has a normal sexual relationship with a woman. Friends and colleagues are generally shocked when this type of offender is discovered. This type of offender does not necessarily plan the abuse; he generally describes it as "something that just happened." Although his primary sexual interest is in other adults, he finds adolescents less demanding. He is likely to describe his relationship as "loving" (Groth, 1982).

Crosson-Tower (2002) has identified four conditions that must exist before a person molests a child. First is the motivation of the abuser. He is likely to feel an emotional congruence with children, be sexually aroused by children, and have normal sexual outlets blocked. The second precondition is a lack of internal inhibitors. He rationalizes that having sex with a child is normal. Third is a lack of external inhibitors. The child abuser has to have access to the child and opportunity to "groom" the child. This is the reason that coaches, educators, day care workers, and members of the clergy are frequently discovered to be child molesters. This does not mean that people in these professions are more likely to be molesters; it means that molesters are more likely to go into these professions in order to gain access to children. According to Crosson-Tower, the final precondition for child abuse is the abuser's ability to overcome the child's resistance. If the home and the school fail to educate the child about child abuse, if the child has a low self-concept, or if the child has no adults to confide in or trust, he or she is more likely to be a victim of child abuse.

Shakeshaft and Cohan (1995) report that "often the teachers who sexually abuse their students are judged to be among the best teachers in a district and are very popular with the students and parents" (p. 515). They report that allegations of abuse are most likely to be made against staff members who worked with students in extracurricular activities or who had frequent one-to-one contact with students. For instance, "a disproportionate number of accusations were made against coaches and drama, art, music, and gym teachers. . . . Indeed, many of the abusers seem to be teachers whom, before the allegations, parents hoped their children would get" (p. 516).

"The vast majority (96%) of the abusers in [their] study were males. Of the students the males sexually abused, 76% were female and 24% were male. Of the students the females sexually abused, 86% were female and 14% were male" (p. 516). Shakeshaft and Cohan classified educator sexual abuse as either non-contact or contact sexual abuse. They further divided the classifications into two levels. Level I non-contact sexual abuse includes such actions as exhibitionism, showing sexually explicit pictures, or making gestures. "Level II non-contact sexual abuse includes making sexual comments, jeering or taunting, and asking questions about sexual activity. Level I contact sexual abuse involves fondling, touching, stroking, and kissing and includes touching students on the outside of their clothes, touching them on the breasts or buttocks, and sexual hugging and kissing. Level II contact sexual abuse includes genital touching, vaginal or anal insertion and oral/genital contact" (p. 515).

MISCONCEPTIONS ABOUT CHILD ABUSERS

Homosexuality

Social science research does not support the claim that gay men and lesbians are more likely than, or even as likely as, straight men or women to sexually abuse children. When an adult male abuses a female child the problem is not heterosexuality, and similarly, when an adult male abuses a male child, the problem is not homosexuality. Some people seem to confuse homosexuality, the attraction to adults of the same sex, with pedophilia, the sexual attraction to children. In fact, two studies that examined the sexual orientation of child molesters found that gays and lesbians may be *less* likely than heterosexuals to sexually abuse children. As Finkelhor (1994) reports,

> because most child molesters are men, some have argued that homosexuals abuse children at a rate higher than their proportion of the general population. Such claims are based on the false belief that men who sexually abuse boys are homosexual. In fact, the overwhelming majority of men who sexually abuse children live their lives as heterosexual men. (p. 31)

Stevenson (2000) reviewed the existing social science literature on the relationship between sexuality and child sexual abuse and found that "a gay man is no more likely than a straight man to perpetrate sexual activity with children" (p. 8). Further, "cases of perpetration of sexual behavior with a pre-pubescent child by an adult lesbian are virtually nonexistent" (p. 8).

In a review of 352 medical records of children evaluated for sexual abuse during a twelve-month period, Jenny and Roesler (1994) found that less than one percent of the abused children were abused by a gay man or a lesbian. Of 269 adult perpetrators of child abuse identified among the 352 cases of abuse, only two (or 0.07 percent) were gay or lesbian. They noted that the vast majority of the children in the sample (82 percent) "were suspected of being abused by a man or a woman who was, or had been, in a heterosexual relationship with a relative of the child" (p. 42). They concluded that in this sample, "a child's risk of being molested by his or her relative's heterosexual partner is over 100 times greater than by someone who might be identifiable as being homosexual, lesbian, or bisexual" (p. 42).

A 1978 study of men convicted of child molestation found none of the 175 men had an exclusively homosexual adult sexual orientation. The study suggested that "fixated" pedophiles are attracted to "the child's immature body type or lack of secondary sex characteristics rather than the child's gender" (Groth & Birnbaum, 1978, p. 180). Almost half (47 percent) of the men in the Massachusetts study were classified as "fixated," 40 percent as "regressed adult heterosexuals," and the other 13 percent as "regressed adult bisexuals" (p. 180). The men classified as regressed adult bisexuals had primary sexual attractions to women. In this last group, Groth and Birnbaum observed,

> in their adult relationships they engaged in sex on occasion with men as well as with women. However, in no case did this attraction to men exceed their preference for women . . . there were no men who were primarily sexually attracted to other adult males. (p. 180)

Females Who Sexually Exploit Children

The sexual abuse of a child by a woman was once thought to be so rare it could be ignored. Consequently, countless studies have analyzed male sex offenders, but only in the past couple of years have efforts been made to study their female counterparts. "As a result the damage that female sex offenders do to the lives of their victims is often underestimated. Many get away with their crimes—and those who are caught often receive comparatively light sentences" (Pochna, 2002).

The thought of women sexually exploiting children strikes at the core of society's view of women as nurturers, caregivers, and protectors. Hendrie (1998) reports that cases "in which female educators are cast in the culturally unfamiliar role of sexual predator, pose special challenges for schools, courts, and communities alike" (p. 13). She believes the emotional dynamics in the case of a female molester are often notably different from cases involving men. Such cases challenge any number of social stereotypes: "Women are victims, not predators; boys who have sex with older women should consider themselves lucky; and love justifies even the most unlikely of matches" (p. 14).

Both men and women can behave inappropriately, and young boys are just as vulnerable to abuse as young girls. Hendrie (1998) suggests that women play a significant, if decidedly secondary, role in sexual exploitation. Her research revealed nearly 250 cases of alleged staff-on-student sexual misconduct. She reports that nearly one in five involved female employees. "In five of those cases, the victims were girls. The rest were boys in middle or high school, ranging in age from 11 to 17" (p. 14). (For a detailed discussion of two cases of female teachers sexually exploiting male students, see the Introduction.)

Patterns Vary by Gender

The dynamics of staff-on-student sex vary depending on the sex of the participants. For example, women seldom use force to compel sex or threaten victims to keep them silent. They are less likely to deny their actions, and tend to commit such offenses later in life. Women who sexually abuse minors generally were sexually molested as children, are coerced to take part in such abuse by men, or fall in love with a youngster they supervise or teach.

Both men and women seem to believe that because young male victims often freely agree to sex, they are not being harmed. Most male school employees who sexually exploit students do not have a romantic attachment to their victims. Men in such cases tend to justify their relationships by saying the girls were willing sex partners. However, their female victims often say that they fell in love with their teacher. Additionally, it is far more common for men to exploit a series of students over time. Such behavior is rare among women.

You Be the Judge: Chapter 6 Scenario

Candi is a shy ninth-grader who is not very athletic and does not get very good grades. She does not have many friends and does not like school. However, she is thrilled when her math teacher asks her to be his student worker. She goes to the teacher's classroom during her study halls and helps him grade papers. Recently, she has begun staying after school to help the teacher organize material for his personal business. When the teacher starts talking with her about his marriage, she is flattered. When he tells her how mature she is and how much he enjoys being around her, she tells him she likes being with him also. After a six-month sexual relationship, the teacher tells Candi that he can't see her anymore. Candi becomes despondent and attempts suicide.

1. Could a similar scenario take place in your school district?

2. Did sexual exploitation occur in this scenario? Why or why not?

3. Do you need more information to answer the above questions? If so, what other information do you need?

4. Who, if anyone, would likely be liable?

5. What could have been done to prevent this incident?

7

District and Employee Rights and Responsibilities

DISTRICT RIGHTS AND RESPONSIBILITIES

Lawsuits brought against school districts that stem from allegations of educator sexual exploitation are generally based on one of two legal theories. Either the district is sued for the negligent acts of the employee under the doctrine of *respondeat superior,* or it is sued for negligent hiring, retention, or supervision. In the negligent hiring, retention, or supervision cases, the district is not being sued for the actual sexual exploitation, but for its alleged failure to properly screen the candidate, failure to provide proper instruction about appropriate behavior, failure to adequately supervise, or failure to take prompt and appropriate action when it knew of the offense.

Respondeat Superior/Vicarious Liability

Because school districts are purely legal entities and cannot actually act or intend an action, the courts focus on the employees of the district as a means of imputing the guilty act to the district. This concept is based on the doctrine of *respondeat superior.* This doctrine states that a master is liable in certain circumstances for the negligent acts of his servant, provided the negligent acts occurred in the course of his employment (Lienhard, 1996). Courts have generally held the employer liable only for actions that are outrageous, are motivated by personal interests, or do not serve a rational business purpose, or where the employer deliberately remained ignorant of criminal conduct.

John R., then a 14-year-old junior high school student, was allegedly sexually molested by his mathematics teacher while participating in an officially sanctioned extracurricular program. John's parents brought suit against the teacher and the district, alleging that the district was vicariously liable for the teacher's acts and directly liable for negligence. The principle question before the court was whether the school district that employed the teacher was vicariously liable for the teacher's acts under the doctrine of *respondeat superior.* The court ruled that while the school district may be liable if its own direct negligence is established, it cannot be held vicariously liable for its employee's torts (*John R. v. Oakland*, 1989).

The court said that to assume that the school district could foresee the abuse would "reflect an unduly pessimistic view of human nature, [suggesting] . . . that sexual misconduct is foreseeable any time a minor and an adult are alone in a room together, at least if not constrained by the possibility of being interrupted." The court differentiated between an act being conceivable, and being foreseeable. Therefore, the court characterized the teacher's abuse of the child as "so unusual or startling that vicarious liability cannot fairly be imposed on the district." The court agreed that although it is "unquestionably important to encourage both the careful selection of these employees and the close monitoring of their conduct, such concerns are, we think, better addressed by holding school districts to the exercise of due care in such matters and subjecting them to liability only for their own direct negligence in that regard" (*John R. v. Oakland*, 1989). Consequently, to recover under *respondeat superior,* the plaintiff must demonstrate that the employee's acts were committed within the scope of his employment.

Parents have successfully argued that the school district should be liable for the conduct of its employee when the district had actual knowledge of the exploitation. This theory only applies when the employee is acting within the scope of his or her employment. Consequently, if the actions of the employee serve his or her own purposes and not those of the employer, the employee would be acting outside the scope of his or her employment. Generally, employee sexual exploitation is considered to be outside the scope of employment.

DeMitchell (2002) argues that courts have consistently shielded school districts from *respondeat superior* liability in cases of educator sexual exploitation because they have failed to "appreciate that school employees are aided in their misconduct by the power and authority they have over children given to them by virtue of their school employment and its attendant in loco parentis status."

Negligent Hiring, Retention, Assignment, Supervision, or Training

Negligent hiring, retention, assignment, and training are all torts that are based on the premise that schools have a common law duty to protect their students. They are expected to use reasonable care to select employees who are competent to do the work assigned to them. Negligent hiring is a doctrine of primary liability, holding the employer liable for its acts, in contrast to the legal theory of *respondeat superior*, which holds the employer liable for acts of its employees. In order for a determination of negligent hiring to be made, it first must be determined that the employee was negligent. Second, it must be shown that the school was negligent in hiring that individual.

Liability is generally determined by answering the "but for" causation-in-fact test. In other words, if the district owed a duty to hire a competent person, and if negligence is demonstrated, the next question is "Did the harm occur because of the negligence of the employer?" This is often referred to as proximate cause. Was there a natural, direct, and continuous link between the negligent act and the plaintiff's injury? For example, if a school district hired a person who had been convicted of child molestation and placed a 13-year-old female in his band class, and the teacher molested the child, a case can be made for "but for" causation. On the other hand, if a school district conducts a thorough background check, and the teacher rapes a youngster from another school in the parking lot of the mall, there is probably not a "but for" causation. The issue is whether the school should have been able to anticipate that an employee would cause harm.

Generally, negligent hiring or retention cases involve acts that occurred during working hours while the employee was doing his or her job. However, an employer may be found negligent if it can be shown that the plaintiff and the employee would not have come into contact if not for the employment relationship. For example, extracurricular activities, field trips, and sponsored trips could involve negligent hiring or retention. However, there comes a point when the event is so distant from the employment relationship in time and place that the responsibility for adequate supervision lies with the parents.

The theory of negligent hiring is based on the assumption that an employer whose employees are in contact with the public in the course of their employment must exercise reasonable care in the selection and retention of its employees. In 1982, the Supreme Court of New Jersey explained that a "majority of jurisdictions that have addressed this issue have concluded that an employer who negligently either hires or retains in his employ an individual who is incompetent or unfit for the job, may be liable to a third party whose injury was proximately caused by the employer's negligence" (*DiCosala v. Kay*, 1982).

A cause of action related to negligent hiring is negligent retention. An allegation of negligent hiring argues that the employer knew or should have known the employee was unfit before he or she was employed, while an allegation of negligent retention argues that during the course of employment the employer became aware that the employee was unfit. Courts also recognize negligent assignment and negligent training as related causes of action.

Background Checks

Schools, day care centers, sports programs, and other organizations are increasingly using various services to check on the backgrounds of prospective employees, as a tool to protect children. For example, the National Alliance for Youth Sports (NAYS) believes that background checks are "critical for ensuring well-being of youngsters participating in youth sports programs" (National Alliance for Youth Sports, n.d.).

A comprehensive system of background checking, consistently followed, not only provides increased protection for the students, but also bolsters the district's defense should it face a claim of negligent hiring.

Background checks are one tool to help a school district weed out individuals with criminal backgrounds involving children. School officials should have a clear understanding of the information that will and will not be found when running a background check. For example, a criminal background check will not identify mental disorders. Consequently, employers must regularly talk with employees so they can better detect potential problems.

Schools must cultivate a climate in which staff members will report suspicious or improper behavior. Although background checks serve a purpose, they are only a supplement to a careful screening process that includes a careful evaluation of all other supporting documents. Each applicant should be asked to submit letters of reference. All work experience should be carefully verified. Every candidate should be specifically asked if he or she has ever been charged with child molestation or if he or she was under any type of investigation when he left any employment.

Screening programs should be integrated into a comprehensive pre-employment process. School districts should develop a pre-employment questionnaire that asks specific questions about the candidate's involvement in criminal activity. Abusers, like any other criminals, move to locations with the easiest targets. If they know a school district is doing background checks, it is less likely that they will apply.

Fingerprinting

Fingerprinting is increasingly being incorporated into the screening process. "More than half the states now have sexual assault laws covering educators who abuse their positions of trust by having sex with students. In 42 states, applicants for state certification are required to undergo criminal-background screenings that involve fingerprint checks through the Federal Bureau of Investigation and the state police" (Hendrie, 2003).

There is a danger that mandatory fingerprinting is a cosmetic solution to a complex problem. Although some teacher associations resist finger-printing as a violation of privacy rights, an increasing number of districts believe that background checks help protect children and are not a significant infringement of educator Fourth Amendment rights.

Failure to Warn

Increasingly, plaintiffs are bringing suits against school districts alleging that the district that formerly employed the educator failed to warn the current employer about allegations of abuse. A California case illustrates the current judicial thinking on this matter. The case concerned letters of recommendation that school district officers allegedly wrote. Randi W. claimed that the school district unreservedly recommended an educator for employment without disclosing to prospective employers that they knew complaints of sexual misconduct had been leveled against him. The receiving school district argued that they were induced to hire the educator, who later sexually assaulted Randi W. The Supreme Court concluded that the defendants' letters of recommendation, containing unreserved and unconditional praise for the former employee despite the defendants' alleged knowledge of complaints of sexual misconduct with students, constituted misleading statements that could form the basis for tort liability for fraud or negligent misrepresentation. Ordinarily a recommending employer is not held accountable to third persons for failing to disclose negative information regarding a former employee. Nonetheless, liability may be imposed if the recommendation letter amounts to an affirmative misrepresentation presenting a foreseeable and substantial risk of physical harm to a third person. The Supreme Court ruled that the defendants could foresee that, had they not unqualifiedly recommended the former employee, the receiving district would not have hired him. And finally, the defendants could foresee that the former employee might molest or injure a student such as the plaintiff (*Randi W. v. Murdoc*, 1997).

Nondisclosure Provisions: "Mobile Molesters"

Justin's story illustrates the consequences of failing to warn. Justin reported that his coach would get him out of his school classes, take him to an empty classroom, get behind him, and rub his shoulders. Justin said he was too frightened to say anything. He reported that the coach kept on "trying to touch me and he put his hand over my privates and said do you want me to touch you here. . . . I didn't want to back-talk him, he's my coach. . . . I'm supposed to respect this guy. I didn't know what to do" (Goldberg & Winn, 2001). The coach was convicted of indecency with a child. What makes Justin's story particularly distressing is the fact that the coach's previous principal had written the coach a letter that said, "numerous complaints have been received concerning you looking at girls' breasts, behinds, and up their skirts. Inappropriate touching of students is also a complaint. Some students have expressed a fear of being alone with you in the classroom." This coach was allowed to resign and apply for a coaching position in another state. The sending district did not tell the receiving district about the allegations. In fact, as part of a negotiated settlement, they wrote him a letter of recommendation. This is a classic example of how a "mobile molester" gets passed from one district to another. This all-too-common situation is often referred to as "passing the trash." Justin's mother was asked what she thought when she learned that this coach's previous employer did not tell the new employer what they knew about him. She replied, "The sending district had to know it was going to happen again" (Goldberg & Winn, 2001).

Generally, nondisclosure agreements contain a provision that allows the employee to resign and prevents the employer from disclosing negative information about the employee. Consequently, future employers considering hiring the district's former employee may be unable to obtain essential information about the employee's fitness to teach. While these agreements may not always be illegal, they are always wrong. Such agreements conceal information from both the local community and prospective employers. Additionally, they often violate state child abuse reporting laws. Not only do nondisclosure agreements permit an employee to resign rather than be dismissed, they conceal the reason that the employee left. There are several reasons school districts give for entering into these agreements: (a) they fear that if they terminate the educator without proof of wrongdoing, the educator will initiate costly due process litigation; (b) although there are rumors and suspicions of inappropriate behavior, the district does not believe it has enough evidence to dismiss the educator; (c) the district fears that if the employee's behavior becomes public, parents will initiate litigation against the district; or (d) the district wishes to avoid negative local publicity regarding the behavior of one of its employees.

> Some states have taken steps to curb the problem known as 'passing the trash': the practice of allowing employees suspected of wrongdoing to leave quietly for new jobs, often to abuse more students. Seventeen states report that they required local school officials to inform the state if educators leave their jobs amid suspicions of sexual misconduct. (Hendrie, 2003)

Letters of Reference

Writing a letter of reference sometimes places school administrators on the horns of a dilemma. On the one hand, they feel a professional responsibility to prevent incompetent or immoral educators from gaining future employment. On the other hand, they fear being sued for defamation by a former employee who does not get a job because of a negative letter of reference.

Former employees who bring defamation suits argue that the negative reference contained false statements that injured the employee's reputation. These suits allege that the former employer impugned the former employee's ability or fitness to teach. Generally, in order to promote candid and open communication, employers are protected by a form of qualified or conditional privilege. This privilege does not protect the employer who provides information that is known to be false or who acts with reckless disregard for the truth or falsity of the information (Restatement, 1977).

Because of the fear of being sued for defamation, some districts are refusing to provide any substantive information about former employees. Ironically, at the same time some school districts are refusing to provide candid information on employees departing their employ, they are seeking information about prospective employees. In an attempt to foster honest communication and discourage frivolous lawsuits, most states have enacted some form of reference immunity statute.

EDUCATOR RIGHTS AND RESPONSIBILITIES

Educators are becoming increasingly concerned that false accusations will destroy their careers, or that innocent behavior will be misconstrued. Increasingly, these fears have resulted in educators refusing to take on the extra responsibilities of sponsoring clubs, tutoring students after school, or coaching teams. Although few youngsters make false allegations of sexual abuse, it would be naive to think that there are no false complaints.

Increasingly, school districts are taking swift action against alleged exploiters as part of their zero-tolerance policies. Educators are concerned that there is a presumption of guilt and a rush to judgment. Believing that educators are not being treated fairly, some educators report that morale has plummeted.

An Educator's Good Name

It is a long-standing legal premise that people should be allowed to protect their reputations and to receive damages as redress when their reputations are harmed. However, in the case of an innocent educator, even when justice is eventually served the reputation of the educator is often irrevocably damaged.

Defamation of Character

Educators accused of exploitation are using the anti-defamation laws to defend themselves against allegedly unwarranted accusations. On the one hand, a defamation suit may be a legitimate strategy on the part of an innocent educator to rehabilitate his or her reputation. On the other hand, it appears that some educators accused of sexual exploitation use the threat of a defamation suit to intimidate the victim. In the past, educators who believed they were the victims of groundless accusations would often quietly resign and leave the profession. Recently, educators have become more assertive in defending themselves. Because it takes so much courage to come forward, advocates of victims of abuse believe defamation suits will have a chilling effect on victims.

Defamation is the "holding up of a person to ridicule, scorn or contempt in a respectable and considerable part of the community" (*Black's Law Dictionary*, 1999). If the defamation suit concerns a written attack, it is libel; if it concerns a verbal assault, it is slander. Defamation is an untruth, communicated to a third party, that does harm. The standard of proof is different if the plaintiff is a "public official" than if he is a "private citizen." It is more difficult for a public official to win a defamation suit because he must show the statements were made with the intention to do harm. Private citizens do not have to prove actual malice. Unfortunately, courts are not uniform in their holdings regarding the standing of educators. For example, in a Virginia case involving a newspaper article that alleged that an educator was "disorganized, erratic, forgetful, and unfair," the court held that educators are private citizens. The court further ruled that the newspaper had a duty to investigate the truth of the statements. A jury awarded the teacher $100,000 in compensatory damages (*Richmond Newspapers v. Lipscomb*, 1987). However, in a Tennessee case that grew out of a newspaper report that implied a teacher was a child molester, the court ruled that the teacher was a public official. Consequently, the court focused on the intent of the publisher rather than the truth of the statement (*Campbell v. Robinson*, 1997). If the educator is regarded as a public official, he or she will have an uphill battle to win a defamation case.

Public officials receive less protection than private individuals when publicly criticized. Consequently, if educators seek public attention or invite some sort of notoriety, they may achieve the status of a public official. Coaches are generally treated as public figures (Markovitz, 2000).

Educator Due Process

When an educator has tenure, he or she can be dismissed only for good cause, and not for reasons which are arbitrary, capricious, or irrelevant. Good cause generally falls into one of three broad categories: insubordination, incompetence, or immorality. Immorality as a ground for dismissal may include a broad range of conduct. Sexual misconduct is the most frequent subset of immorality. An educator's personal conduct cannot serve as grounds for dismissal unless there is a connection between the conduct and the performance of his or her duties. Sexual conduct with a student will almost always support discharge, provided there is sufficient evidence to show that the misconduct occurred. Generally courts have found the effect of immorality to be irremediable. For example, in a case where an educator behaved in a sexually suggestive way toward female students, the court found the behavior damaged the reputation of the faculty and the district, and caused psychological harm to students. Even if it could be shown that the behavior would not be repeated, the court found the behavior irremediable (*Scott County School Dist. No. 2 v. Dietrich*, 1986).

What should happen to an educator while the investigation is being conducted? Regardless of the outcome of an investigation, the educator's career and reputation will likely be significantly damaged as a result of any public allegation of immorality. Consequently, making every effort to provide the educator with every protection until the charges are settled is not only the legally correct thing to do, it is the ethically correct thing to do. There are three issues that must be addressed: safety of the students, due process rights of the educator, and possible defamation charges against the administrator or school.

Liberty Interest

A liberty right involves an individual's right to engage in an occupation, among other things. Consequently, when a school district takes any action that might damage an employee's standing in the community or ability to take advantage of future employment opportunities, a liberty interest is involved.

Although school districts are not prohibited from depriving an individual of liberty rights, the actions must not be arbitrary or capricious, and the employee must be provided with due process.

Taking any action against an employee on the basis of an allegation of immorality would harm the educator's opportunities for future employment. To succeed on a claim of liberty interest infringement, the employee must prove (a) the employee's good name or reputation was harmed by a statement of the school board, (b) the statement was false, and (c) the statement occurred in the course of termination of employment. Generally, an employee is entitled to a "name clearing hearing" if he or she believes that his or her liberty rights have been infringed upon. Even if the school board takes action against an employee in executive session and never makes the allegations public, the employee may have a right to a hearing if rumors about the reason for the termination spread through the community. In most states, an employee's refusal to take advantage of such a hearing disallows the liberty interest claim.

Property Interest

Educators gain property interest in their employment when they receive tenure or a continuing contract. A nontenured educator has property interest only for the term of the contract. Although each state has a statute regarding the specific due process rights of school employees, there are some general components of due process that hold for every state. In cases of liberty or property interests, educators are generally guaranteed the right (a) to have counsel of their own choice present, (b) to present witnesses, (c) to cross-examine the witnesses, (d) to testify, (e) to an orderly hearing, and (f) to a fair and impartial decision based on substantial evidence.

Regardless of the finding of any state agency, a school board has the right to conduct its own investigation to determine if an educator should remain employed. In some cases there may not be enough evidence to satisfy a court of law that abuse has taken place. However, the educator's actions may still fall below the standards of the profession and the school district may decide to dismiss the teacher. Accused educators often argue that a school board cannot conduct an impartial hearing. However, the majority of courts have ruled that boards of education can both investigate an allegation and conduct the hearing. Courts presume that school boards act with honesty and integrity.

Suspension With or Without Pay

In order to protect students and the best interests of the district, the power of suspension is essential to sound administration. This authority is expressly granted to the school board in most states. Because of the potential harm that an exploitative educator could do during the period of investigation, it is imperative that accused educators be relieved of teaching duties. However, a hearing must be held prior to a decision to suspend an educator without pay or terminate an educator's contract.

Generally, the employee may be suspended pending a hearing on the charges and the final determination. In most cases the employee is suspended with pay. However, in some cases school boards have suspended employees without pay. For example, in the case of a tenured counselor who was suspended without pay after being charged with "spending the night at a residence and sleeping with an 18-year-old former student," the school board contended that not withholding compensation during periods of suspension would constitute a gift of public funds. The appeals court ruled "the Board of Education did not have the authority to withhold compensation during the period of suspension of the teacher involved" (*Goldin v. Board of Educ.*, 1974).

DEFENSES THAT HAVE BEEN SUCCESSFUL

Defenses that have succeeded in sexual exploitation cases include the following:

- *No exploitation occurred.* Although it is possible that a complaint is a fabrication by a malicious student, it is critical that all complaints be investigated. If an investigation is completed by the school district or OCR and no evidence of sexual exploitation is found, it is unlikely that the school district will be liable. The burden of proof is on the person bringing the complaint.

- *The incident occurred, but it was not unwelcome.* If the actions were solicited, incited, or encouraged it will be more difficult for the person bringing the complaint to prevail. However, this defense must be used only with extreme care, because the consent may have been given out of fear and therefore would not have been voluntary. It must also be remembered that minors are not legally capable of entering into a consensual relationship with adults. Consequently, even if a student agreed to have sexual intercourse with an educator, it may still be a violation of state laws.

- *The unwanted behavior was not severe.* In order to be sexual harassment, the behavior must be sufficiently severe or pervasive to affect the student's ability to learn, and the behavior must create an abusive environment. In order for the incident to be sexual abuse the state statute must have been violated.

- *The employer had no knowledge of the exploitation.* If it can be demonstrated that the district did not know, and if there was a clearly defined and well-publicized grievance procedure for claims, it is unlikely a court would find the district liable for the sexual harassment.

- *The incident occurred, but the school took prompt and appropriate action.* Upon notice of the complaint, the district must conduct a prompt and thorough investigation. If it is determined that the exploitation took place, there must be prompt punishment commensurate with the severity of the harassment. A prompt investigation and appropriate consequences will make it less likely that a court would find the school district liable. This would especially be true if the school district's actions were also aimed at preventing future incidents of sexual harassment.

DEFENSES THAT HAVE NOT BEEN SUCCESSFUL

Defenses that have not succeeded include the following:

- *The youngster is "crying wolf."* Although there may be false complaints, it is the responsibility of the school to take all complaints seriously and to investigate all complaints.

- *The victim did not make a prompt report.* Many victims of sexual exploitation do not report because they are afraid that they will not be believed, are afraid they will be blamed, don't know how to complain, or fear retaliation. The fact that no formal complaint was filed may not protect a district from a judgment.

- *No real harm resulted.* Often a school district will attempt to dismiss a complaint of sexual exploitation by saying there was no significant harm. This is a question of fact that a court will decide. Generally plaintiffs present medical and educational experts to document any harm.

- *The youngster was "sexually provocative."* Although the behavior, speech, dress, or demeanor of the plaintiff may be admissible in a court proceeding, it is not a defense to a charge of sexual exploitation.

THE AFTERMATH OF A PROVEN ALLEGATION

Educator exploitation harms the child, the child's family, the abuser's family, and the abuser. Additionally, when an educator exploits a student, the crime leaves the school community reeling long after the headlines fade. The child will likely have to deal with long-term consequences. Incidents of sexual exploitation are very traumatic to the entire school community. In order to restore calm and order the school should be sure that

- The victim and his or her family are receiving counseling
- Efforts have been made to identify any unreported victims
- Retaliation is not taking place
- The incident is used as an opportunity to review all policies and procedures to determine what modifications may be needed
- Efforts are renewed to educate everyone about the district's policies and procedures

The district should use the awareness raised by the incident as an opportunity to restate that such behavior will not be tolerated, and highlight the policies that exist.

You Be the Judge: Chapter 7 Scenario

Susan is a high school math teacher and swimming coach. She has taught in the district for over 10 years. There has never been a complaint against her and her evaluations are always high. Two nights a week she works as a swimming instructor at the local fitness club. She is arrested for molesting one of the youngsters in her swimming class. The family of the child sues the school, arguing that because she is a school employee, the school is responsible for her actions.

1. Could a similar scenario take place in your school district?

2. Did sexual exploitation occur in this scenario? Why or why not?

3. Do you need more information to answer the above questions? If so, what other information do you need?

4. Who, if anyone, would likely be liable?

5. What could have been done to prevent this incident?

8

Conducting an Investigation

WHEN SHOULD AN INVESTIGATION BE INITIATED?

All cases of suspected child abuse must be reported to the state's child protection agency or the police. However, many incidents of inappropriate behavior do not cross the threshold into child abuse. For example, hostile environment sexual harassment is a threshold behavior that may develop into child abuse. There are three general circumstances in which the school should conduct its own investigation: (1) when it appears that there is something wrong, but the school does not have enough information to determine whether the behavior was inappropriate; (2) when there is an allegation of inappropriate behavior, but it does not appear to constitute child abuse; or (3) when the school believes that an educator may have behaved unprofessionally, but there is not enough evidence to indicate that a state law has been violated. Each of these three circumstances is problematic. Just because there is not enough evidence for the police or the state agency to take legal action, does not mean that no harm has occurred. In these instances the school district has an obligation to determine whether the behavior violates the school district's policies. The consequences of not conducting an investigation can be quite costly. For example, a South Carolina jury ordered a private school, its headmaster, and its principal to pay $105 million to the father of a victim of a school employee's sexual exploitation after finding that the school failed to investigate the student's reports. The school eventually settled nine other lawsuits relating to the teacher's sexual abuse of over 20 students during his 10 years at the school ("How to Investigate Reports," 2002).

Ross and Marlowe (1985) compare an investigation of educator sexual exploitation to a homicide investigation. At least one of these three elements is needed: a confession, a witness, or strong physical evidence.

According to Shakeshaft and Cohan (1995), most superintendents learn of educator exploitation after the victim's parent contacts the school principal, another staff member, or the police. "In fewer cases, the student, a friend of the student, or the parent of the friend brought the allegations to the attention of the school" (p. 516). In a number of cases, the superintendent had not been informed of previous allegations against the same staff member. Shakeshaft and Cohan indicate that many school districts do not have a well-thought-out procedure for investigating allegations of sexual exploitation. For example, in the school districts they studied, superintendents conducted the initial questioning of the student who was alleging abuse. Some of these students were questioned with their parents, and others were questioned without the parents' knowledge. If the superintendent believed that the allegation had merit, the school attorney, board president, and union president would be informed of what was happening. The superintendent "usually did not contact the police, the district attorney's office, nor did they usually report the allegations to child abuse hot lines" (p. 516). Often the educator's claim that the allegations were untrue or that the behavior had been misconstrued ended the matter. Superintendents took allegations against female educators more seriously than allegations against male educators. "Behaviors that might have resulted in a slap on the wrist for male teachers could result in termination for females" (p. 517). They also found that homosexual acts were viewed as more serious than heterosexual acts. Thus students who reported same-sex exploitation were more likely to be believed and to be judged as harmed more severely than students who reported opposite-sex exploitation.

Anatomy of a Complaint

There are five ways that allegations of sexual exploitation may come to the attention of a school principal: (1) a formal complaint, (2) an informal complaint, (3) observed abuse, (4) observed suspicious behavior, and (5) rumors or anonymous reports (see Figure 8.1). The first three place the school on notice, and the school must either report the suspected abuse to the state child protection agency or conduct an investigation. The last two present a more difficult problem.

Although an educator may not be disciplined based on a rumor or anonymous report, the principal should heighten his or her scrutiny of the accused, and re-educate all staff and students regarding school policy and acceptable and unacceptable behaviors. If an investigation is not initiated,

Figure 8.1 Anatomy of a Sexual Abuse Complaint

Anatomy of a Sexual Abuse Complaint

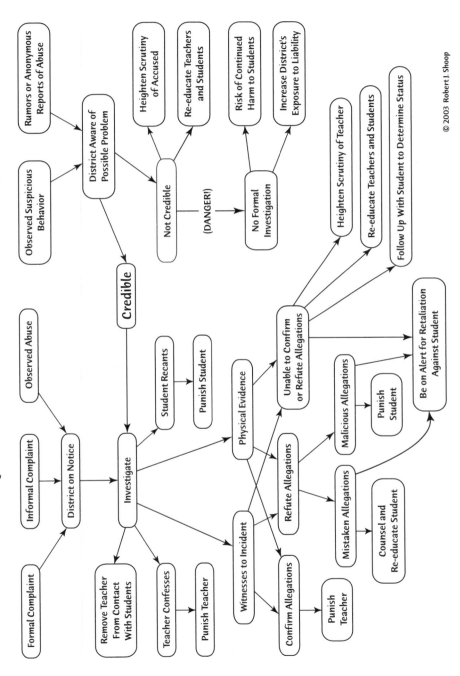

© 2003 Robert J. Shoop

the district runs the risk that the abuse actually occurred. In these cases it is common for the school and the principal to be accused of displaying "deliberate indifference." There are many cases in which courts have awarded damages to plaintiffs who proved that the school was advised that the educator was molesting a student, but failed to take prompt and appropriate action. Of course, the most serious consequence of failing to conduct an investigation is that youngsters may continue to be exploited.

The Purpose of an Investigation

When properly done, an investigation allows the school district to resolve the allegation according to the standards of fairness and due process. A proper investigation also minimizes the risk of the school district being charged with failure to take prompt and appropriate action calculated to protect the alleged victim and other youngsters in the school. The investigation must respect the privacy rights and professional reputation of the accused, and at the same time be thorough and complete. The primary impediments to conducting a successful investigation are (a) excessive delay in beginning the investigation, (b) incomplete investigations, (c) unnecessary or unauthorized disclosure of confidential or privileged information, and (d) lack of skill of the investigator (Ehrlich, 1997).

The first question that must be answered is whether an investigation is called for. Some school administrators are so afraid of not taking a complaint seriously that they initiate an investigation when it is not likely to produce any usable results. For example, a totally anonymous note that says "One of your teachers is a 'dirty old man'" is probably too vague to yield usable information. However, simply because a complaint is unsigned does not mean that it is not worthy of investigation. An unsigned note identifying a specific individual or class should likely warrant an investigation.

On the other hand, some administrators fail to recognize the problem unless a student specifically complains of sexual exploitation. This is especially problematic because many students have not been taught to understand or recognize sexual exploitation. For example, an elementary school student may say "I don't like it when my teacher tickles me." Or a high school student may ask to change his or her class schedule because of a "personality conflict with a teacher." Both of these incidents may indicate that further investigation is warranted.

School districts lose cases if they do not take prompt and appropriate action when sexual exploitation occurs. Courts have ruled against school districts when

- There was no policy, or it was incomplete
- There was no training of staff and students

- There was not a clear grievance procedure
- There was excessive delay at the beginning of the investigation
- Confidential information was disclosed
- Evidence was misinterpreted
- The punishment was not appropriate to the offense
- There was some type of retaliation against the person bringing the complaint

Even when the county attorney or child protection agency decides not to prosecute a case, or when they conclude that child abuse has not occurred, the school district still has a duty to investigate the complaint. For example, a school district lost a civil suit because it abandoned its investigation after the county attorney decided there was not enough evidence to warrant a criminal prosecution. Several months later, the complaint was verified. In the months following the conclusion of the criminal investigation, a number of other students were sexually exploited by the educator who was named in the original complaint.

As long as there have been schools, administrators have faced complaints of improper educator behavior. Upon receiving a report of improper behavior, it was common for the administrator to talk to the alleged victim, talk to the alleged perpetrator, make an "executive decision" as to the validity of the complaint, and dispense punishment. It was not unusual for the administrator to simply tell the educator to stop the inappropriate behavior. Often no investigation was conducted and records were seldom kept.

Just as anxiety can prompt an unnecessary investigation, uncertainty can cause some administrators to hesitate to initiate the investigation. Delaying the start of the investigation is a serious error that may be interpreted as a lack of commitment to the elimination of sexual exploitation. In the case of an investigation that took almost nine months to conclude, the court ruled that the investigation was not conducted in a timely manner.

The investigation should begin promptly upon receipt of a report of suspected misconduct. Some experts believe that having school officials investigate "one of their own" compromises the integrity of the investigation. These experts believe that hired investigators or law enforcement officials should investigate because they're impartial and more experienced in investigating sexual misconduct. Other experts believe that school officials are the best people to investigate sexual misconduct reports because they have access to all the parties involved; may have access to areas where the sexual misconduct took place, if it occurred on school grounds; and may have easy access to physical evidence, such as computers containing e-mail correspondence and visits to chat rooms. Also, because school officials already have relationships with the victim, the employee, and potential witnesses, they may be in a better position than an outside investigator to get these individuals to speak candidly about what happened.

Investigator Training

If the district conducts its own investigation, it must make sure the people conducting the investigation are properly trained. Several designated school employees should be trained in school policy, relevant state and federal laws, and investigation techniques and procedures. Investigators should gather and document all relevant information regarding the suspected misconduct; interview the victim, the suspected employee, and any witnesses; and gather any physical evidence, such as letters, e-mail correspondence, or photographs. It is important to endeavor to keep the names of the alleged victim, suspected exploiter, and any witnesses, as well as the nature of the investigation, confidential. This will minimize attempts to pressure the student to recant the allegations, and may protect the reputation of an innocent employee. However, no promises should be made that the material will be kept confidential.

When Should the Educator Be Removed From Contact With Students?

One of the most important decisions to be made is what to do with the employee during the investigation. In making this decision, the school must balance the rights of the employee, who may be erroneously accused of sexual misconduct, with its duty to protect the student from harm. If the allegations involve improper language, or a nonphysical form of sexual harassment, it may be possible to allow the educator to remain in the classroom during the investigation. However, if the complaint involves sexual intimidation, inappropriate contact, stalking, sexual propositions, or sexual contact, the school has a duty to remove the educator from contact with students.

When in doubt, school administrators should err on the side of protecting the student by removing the suspected employee from contact with students. Depending on the nature of the conduct, and the duties of the suspected employee, the options include changing the employee's duties and suspension.

The Complaint File

All complaints, whether or not they can be substantiated, should be dated and retained in a central file, and reviewed annually to determine whether any trends are developing and to gain a better understanding of the climate of the school. Copies of all relevant school district policies and procedures should be retained for each investigation. This includes copies of board policies, faculty and student handbooks, any training materials, and any newsletters that include discussions of sexual exploitation. Personal comments must be kept out of the report (Ehrlich, 1997).

Figure 8.2 Sexual Harassment/Sexual Exploitation Complaint Form

Name _____   Date _____

School _____

Who was responsible for the harassment or exploitation? _____

Describe the harassment or exploitation. _____
_____
_____
_____

Date, time, and place the harassment or exploitation occurred. _____
_____
_____
_____

List other students or employees involved in the harassment or exploitation. _____
_____
_____
_____

In what way were these other people involved? _____
_____
_____
_____

List any witnesses to the harassment or exploitation. _____
_____
_____
_____

What was your reaction to the harassment or exploitation? _____
_____
_____
_____

Describe any subsequent incidents. _____
_____
_____
_____

Signature of Complainant _____

Date of Report _____

CONDUCTING THE INVESTIGATION

According to Ehrlich (1997), prior to conducting an investigation, the district should ensure that (a) its investigation procedure has been checked against the sexual exploitation policy, any negotiated agreements, and all relevant state laws; (b) the investigators are trained in legal issues relating to sexual exploitation and the procedure for conducting the investigation; (c) consideration is given to training multiple investigation teams; (d) the investigators chosen are well-respected, credible, open-minded, objective, and empathetic; and (e) the investigators understand their responsibilities.

In some cases, the team collects and presents the facts. In other cases, it makes a recommendation for action. It is best that the principal not conduct the investigation. When the allegations are against an educator, other educators and community members will choose sides. Also, if the educator is found innocent, or if there is not enough information to make a determination as to the educator's guilt or innocence, the principal will have to work with him or her after the investigation.

Prior to the start of the investigation, there must be a clear understanding of who will make the ultimate decision concerning whether the abuse took place and what discipline and remedies are appropriate (Ehrlich, 1997).

The first step is to interview the person making the complaint, at which time he or she should be asked to put the complaint in writing. Having a written complaint (a) makes it clear that the school takes the complaint seriously, (b) reduces the likelihood that the student will embellish the report, and (c) provides a structure for conducting the investigation. Although the school is on notice even if the person bringing the complaint refuses to put the complaint in writing, the school district cannot impose sanctions on an employee if the charges are anonymous. During the interview of the complainant, the investigators should determine whether there were any witnesses to the alleged incident(s). The complainant should be interviewed before the alleged abuser is informed of the complaint. There have been cases in which the accused contacted the child before she was interviewed and intimidated her into recanting. The complainant should not be required to have a face-to-face meeting with the accused. Requiring such a meeting may cause the youngster to become too afraid to cooperate.

The complainant should be (a) assured that the complaint is taken seriously, (b) asked to describe in detail the behaviors that he or she found inappropriate or offensive, and (c) asked when and where the incidents took place, and whether there were any witnesses. It is not uncommon for the student to request that no action be taken against the exploiter. He or she may simply want the exploitation to stop. The district must follow its policy regardless of the wishes of the student. The student should be specifically told to report any incidents of retaliation.

After the student is interviewed and the allegations are clarified, the accused school employee should be interviewed. At this time, the accused should be given the opportunity to give his or her version of the events and respond to the allegations. The accused should also be given the opportunity to identify any witnesses to the alleged incident. The accused should be warned about retaliating against the student.

The investigators should then interview all witnesses. In cases where there are no witnesses, conclusions may have to be reached from the first two interviews. Both the complainant and the accused should be informed that they may bring a support person to their interview. Involving the parents or guardians of the student may present some problems. The parents have a right to be with their child. However, it is possible that the child will be embarrassed to speak openly in front of his or her parents. Parents should be asked for permission to speak with the child alone. In some cases, the child may come into the principal's office and begin talking before there is a chance to contact the parent. In this situation, the parents should be contacted as soon as the principal realizes that there is an issue of exploitation.

When the Investigation Is Concluded

Once the investigation is concluded, a report should be written summarizing the information gathered and providing a clear statement of the investigation's results. After the report is filed, the designated body should make a decision and inform both parties of the results of the investigation. The victim and his or her family do not have the right to be told what punishment has been assigned. Generally, the investigator serves as a fact finder and does not determine the consequences of the investigation. The superintendent generally makes a recommendation to the school board, and the board makes the final decision.

Outcomes of the Investigation

The three possible outcomes of an investigation are that (1) the allegation is confirmed, (2) the allegation is refuted, or (3) the allegation cannot be confirmed or refuted (see Figure 8.1). If the allegation is confirmed, the educator must be punished. If the allegation is refuted, the investigators must determine whether the allegation was made because of a misunderstanding or confusion, or whether it was made with malice. In the case of a mistaken allegation, the student should be counseled regarding the harm caused and ways to avoid repeating the mistake. If it is determined that the allegation was made with malice, the student must be punished. However, if the allegation can neither be confirmed nor refuted, the principal must heighten his or her scrutiny of the accused educator. The educator should be counseled about questionable practices and behaviors that might be misconstrued. The principal should follow up with the student to determine whether the problem continues.

There is the very real potential for some form of retaliation against the student bringing a complaint. This retaliation may be instigated by the accused educator or by other students who either do not believe the allegations against the educator or who resent that the educator has been punished. Any form of retaliation is a separate incident of harassment that must be promptly investigated.

False Accusations

The increased attention paid to educator exploitation has generated a predictable reaction from some educators. Some believe that legitimate cases have been sensationalized by the media. This concern has resulted in some educators becoming cynical and defensive. Their fear of false accusations is having a negative impact on their morale. The following statements are representative of educator reactions after training sessions: "How can I protect myself against a false complaint?" "What happens to a teacher if a student lies about abuse?" "Just being accused of abusing a student is the 'kiss of death.'" "Are students who file a false complaint punished?" A veteran teacher recently said, "Our school district has a new policy that states, 'the only permitted physical contact between teachers and students is a handshake.' This is stupid, and I resent the implication. A few bad teachers are destroying the reputations of the rest of us."

On the one hand, there must be zero tolerance for all forms of sexual exploitation. On the other hand, every effort must be made to protect the reputations of innocent educators. It is important to recognize that a false allegation will significantly damage an educator's reputation and may destroy his or her career. Once the rumor of abuse begins to circulate, the harm may be done.

Shakeshaft and Cohan (1995) report that "7.5% of the superintendents reported that some allegations turned out to be untrue or that the super-intendents had decided that, though the behaviors had occurred, they were not serious enough to be considered sexual abuse" (p. 518). However, Shakeshaft and Cohan believe that "it is more likely that students will fail to report actual incidents than that they will fabricate incidents" (p. 514).

Unfounded Reports Versus False Reports

It is misleading and inaccurate to confuse unfounded reports with false reports. When an investigation concludes that a report is unfounded, it is generally because the investigators do not have adequate data on which to base a decision. Other reports are determined to be unfounded when it is learned that the symptoms that were suggestive of abuse can be attributed to other causes. The findings of a 1987 study indicated that, of 576 cases of sexual abuse that were analyzed, only 1.5 percent were ficti-tious reports made by a child (Kalichman, 1993).

Complete the Investigation

Frequently an educator will resign while under investigation. It is a serious error for the school to discontinue its investigation upon the resignation of the teacher. The school has a duty to find out what happened and provide assistance to any victims of abuse. Also, the school must not do anything to conceal the fact that the educator resigned while under investigation.

ACTIONS TO PROTECT EDUCATORS

The ultimate goal of a prevention program is to create a school that is free of fear, harassment, discrimination, violence, and abuse. The following actions will assist the process:

- *Implement a code of conduct.* The code should explicitly state that all romantic or sexual relationships between students and educators, regardless of the student's age, are prohibited. Educators and students must be taught what constitutes sexual misconduct. They must be taught about boundaries and the difference between acceptable and unacceptable interaction between educators and students.

- *Include prohibition against false complaints.* A specific prohibition against making a false complaint is a step toward protecting the reputation of innocent educators. Students must understand the damage that can be done by a false allegation, and the severe punishment that will be meted out to any student who makes a false complaint. However, if a student recants an allegation, the principal must be sure that the student has not been threatened or suffered retaliation. In the case of a false allegation, the punishment must be strong enough to make it clear that making a false complaint is a very serious matter. The educator should be reinstated and efforts must be made to rehabilitate his or her reputation. Every effort should be made to keep the facts of the incident and the names of the student and educator confidential. However, a falsely accused educator deserves the right to a statement of exoneration.

- *Provide training in prevention strategies.* Specific training is necessary in order to reduce confusion about appropriate and inappropriate physical contact with students. For example, if a third-grade child falls and cuts her knee while running across the playground, most parents would want the teacher to bend down, give her a hug, and tell her she is going to be OK. However, if a parent saw a teacher in the back of a deserted classroom hugging her daughter, it would likely trigger alarm bells of concern. If a high school student won a scholarship, got a new job, or did particularly well on a test, it would be natural for a teacher to pat the student on the back or put an arm over the student's shoulder and offer a side-to-side hug of congratulations. However, regularly hugging students as a form of greeting is not appropriate.

Although some educators may say "I am just a physical person," "students need affection," or "the hug was completely innocent," it is the impact of the action, not the intent, that must be considered. The student may not wish to be hugged, but may be uncomfortable telling an educator to stop. Additionally, observers may misconstrue the educator's behavior. When in doubt, it is prudent to err on the side of caution.

Students must be taught that they have a right to tell an educator if any touch or other behavior makes them uncomfortable. They also have the right to complain to the principal if the educator refuses to stop the unwanted or inappropriate behavior. Regardless of the educator's motivation, when told to stop he or she must discontinue the activity.

You Be the Judge: Chapter 8 Scenario

A principal receives an allegation that a teacher in his school is having a sexual relationship with one of his students. The principal reports the suspected child abuse to the state child protection agency. After an investigation, the state agency informs the principal that the allegation cannot be confirmed or refuted. The county attorney reports that there is not enough evidence to file a charge against the teacher. The principal talks with the teacher and the teacher indicates that the youngster was receiving poor grades and is just trying to make trouble for him because she is angry. The principal makes a note of the allegation on his computer scheduler. Several months later, a youngster goes to the police and reports that she has been having a sexual relationship with the teacher for the past year.

1. Could a similar scenario take place in your school district?

2. Did sexual exploitation occur in this scenario? Why or why not?

3. Do you need more information to answer the above questions? If so, what other information do you need?

4. Who, if anyone, would likely be liable?

5. What could have been done to prevent this incident?

9

Action Steps

A safe school is a place where students learn and educators teach in a welcoming environment, free from intimidation, fear, and exploitation. The following action steps will contribute to eradicating all forms of sexual exploitation. (To assess your school's prevention level, see Appendix D.)

ACTION STEPS FOR SCHOOL DISTRICTS

Policy Prohibiting Sexual Exploitation

A policy prohibiting sexual exploitation should specifically describe inappropriate behaviors and make it clear that no form of sexual exploitation will be tolerated. Having a policy and disseminating it widely documents that the school district has taken reasonable steps to prevent sexual exploitation and will take prompt and effective action to investigate any complaints. The policy must have enough detail to avoid confusion about appropriate and inappropriate behavior, and should include a separate sexual exploitation reporting procedure. The policy should be regularly reviewed to ensure that it is in conformity with any changes in state or federal laws. A signed statement from each employee and student attesting that they have read and understand the policy should be kept on file. The school board should convene a community meeting to inform parents and other community members that the district does not tolerate any form of sexual exploitation. The policy and its educational efforts should be regularly featured in newsletters. (See Appendix A for suggested procedures to follow in developing a sexual exploitation prevention program, and Appendix B for a model sexual exploitation prevention policy.)

Carefully Screen and Select All New Employees

A comprehensive screening protocol will send a very clear message to all current and prospective staff members that inappropriate behaviors will not be tolerated. The board of education must ensure that the staff who are responsible for employment recommendations ask the right questions. Each candidate for employment should be asked if he or she has ever been convicted of any form of sexual exploitation. Because some school districts still allow educators to resign prior to the completion of an investigation, it is necessary to ask the former employer about any unresolved investigations at the time of the candidate's departure.

Several states have developed procedures to assist school districts in the screening process. For example, Arizona maintains a secured, password-protected Web site as a resource for all schools in the state. The Web site provides school districts with current certification information, fingerprint clearance card information, information on ongoing investigations of immoral or unprofessional conduct, and information on any past disciplinary actions taken by the state board. It also allows the schools to report immoral or unprofessional misconduct to the state board via e-mail (Arizona Department of Education, 2003).

Revise All Handbooks

While student and staff handbooks may once have been little more than a means for a school district to set down its rules, today these handbooks are frequently the focus of attention when schools are called upon to defend their actions in court. Increasingly, lawsuits brought against schools allege the school failed to inform parents, students, or faculty members regarding the rules and expectations of the school district. Although there are limits to what rules can do, every faculty and student handbook should specifically state that fraternization between students and staff members is strictly prohibited. (See Appendix B for an example of an anti-fraternization policy.)

Courts do not expect school policies to have mathematical precision (*Turner v. South-Western City Sch. Dist.*, 1999). However, they do expect that a person of ordinary intelligence will be able to interpret the rules. For example, if a district is going to suspend or terminate an employee, the district must provide the employee with notice of the rule or policy that was violated. The more narrowly the policy is defined, the more likely it will be upheld by a court.

Printing the anti-exploitation policy in all handbooks ensures that parents, staff, and students all have the same information. After conducting an extensive examination of student handbooks and court rulings regarding student disciplinary rules, Sansom and Kemerer (2002) concluded that all rules must (a) have a clear purpose, (b) be written so students can understand them, (c) be carefully worded and applied, (d) be made known to students, and (e) be consistently but not mechanically enforced.

Centralize Record Keeping

Establishing a uniform system of incident reporting and record keeping is essential. Districts must be able to keep track of complaints from year to year and from building to building. Threshold behaviors that may not appear to be critical when seen as isolated events may stimulate heightened scrutiny when seen collectively. Consider this hypothetical example: A parent told an assistant principal that Mr. Jones was "becoming too friendly with female students." That same year, several female students told a counselor Mr. Jones made them "feel uncomfortable in class." The principal noticed that Mr. Jones's car was often in the school parking lot after all other teachers had left. The next year Mr. Jones transferred to another school in the same district. Several educators noticed and commented on the fact that Mr. Jones placed posters over the outside windows to his room and over the window in the door. Early in the semester, the assistant principal noticed that an unusually high number of female students asked to transfer out of Mr. Jones's class. Later in the semester, an assistant principal began hearing rumors that Mr. Jones was "dating a student." The police discovered Mr. Jones having sexual intercourse with a student in a parked car. Mr. Jones was arrested, convicted, and incarcerated. The parents sued the district, alleging that it had enough information to take action. Yet no one in the district had more than a glimpse of Mr. Jones's activities. If the school district had a system by which all reports of inappropriate behavior were maintained in one office, it is likely that someone would have intervened before Mr. Jones molested the student.

Require Training for All Employees

All staff and students should participate in training regarding the content and implications of the anti-exploitation policy, the state reporting laws, the causes and consequences of sexual exploitation, and specific strategies for preventing and eliminating sexual exploitation. Incorporate a life skills curriculum that focuses on helping students take increased responsibility for their own safety, and focuses on appropriate educator-student relationships, good decision making, and responsible citizenship. The program should emphasize improving each child's self-concept and value as a person and a student. Initiate a parent education program that not only encourages parents to talk with their children about what is occurring at school, but offers them some specific skills for doing this. Use every complaint as an opportunity to re-educate all students and staff regarding their rights and responsibilities under the policy.

Require Training for All Students

Youngsters must be taught to look for two categories of warning signs that may indicate an exploitation problem exists: "those which are often specifically associated with sexual activity and appear to lead directly to subsequent sexual boundary violations, and those which are not specifically sexual in nature but have been observed to be harbingers of subsequent sexual boundary violations" (Friedman & Boumil, 1995, p. 59).

The nonsexual warning signs include the educator (a) trying to move the relationship to a personal friendship, (b) telling the student his or her personal problems, (c) discouraging the student from talking with other school employees, or (d) asking the student to run personal errands or do other personal favors. These nonsexual activities are efforts to determine the degree to which the exploiter can influence the student. Once the exploiter determines that the student will do whatever is asked, the exploiter will have confidence to move on to the more overtly sexual activities.

Specific sexual warnings may include the educator (a) taking an unusual interest in sexual matters, (b) taking pleasure in hearing about the student's relationship with his or her boyfriend or girlfriend, (c) engaging in seductive behaviors and making sexual jokes or references, (d) suggesting meeting outside of the school environment for a meal or drinks, (e) becoming sexually aroused, (f) scheduling appointments in the evening or when the school is otherwise empty, (g) recommending alcohol or drugs as a means of relaxing, (h) initiating physical contact through standing too close, (i) touching or other contact that appears not to be accidental, and finally (j) suggesting a sexual relationship (Friedman & Boumil, 1995).

Students should be taught that educators who cross the boundaries do so in a very insidious manner. The process of grooming starts with seemingly innocuous behaviors and gradually increases in intensity. Some students who have been sexually exploited by educators report that they cannot tell exactly when the abuse began. This is understandable because many of the initial behaviors are so subtle that unless the students are warned to look for them they will not see them. These behaviors may or may not indicate that a sexual advance is coming. However, by the time overtly sexual behavior begins, it is difficult for the student to confront the educator. If confronted, most molesters will not pursue the grooming and will likely move on to another, less assertive student. Students should be encouraged to tell their parents or the principal if any activity makes them feel uncomfortable. The most dangerous course of action for students is to remain silent. Even if the youngster is able to extract him- or herself from the clutches of the abuser, keeping silent allows the molester to move on to another child (Shoop, 2002).

ACTION STEPS FOR PRINCIPALS

The principal must make it clear that all staff members are expected to be on alert for signs of possible exploitation. All classrooms should have windows that allow natural supervision. Surveillance cameras should be installed in all difficult-to-supervise public areas. Parents should be welcome to visit the school unannounced at any time. All of the school's off-campus sites should be informed about the district's sexual exploitation prevention policy.

Acknowledge That Exploitation May Exist

Every competent administrator should be very aware of the danger of sexual exploitation of students. Research published in educational journals as well as the popular press makes it clear that abusers are often "the last person you would expect." Consequently, administrators must be extremely sensitive to circumstances that could lead to sexual exploitation.

Pay Attention

Competent administrators are skilled at collecting information needed to solve problems. The quality of the information collected depends on their ability to look below the surface. They must continuously scan the environment for information. This includes making daily observations in the school, asking questions, and looking for problems. All rumors, whispers, and oblique complaints must be taken seriously. The principal must make it clear to all students and staff members that he or she wants to know what is going on in the building.

Don't Allow Bias to Cause Judgment Errors

Bias is a systematic, directional tendency to make choices that violate the rules of logic. For example, a competent administrator would know that (a) sexual exploitation is very serious, (b) some educators sexually exploit students, and (c) often the educator that exploits his or her students is the one who seems to be above suspicion, and may be in a position of power or authority. In this situation, an example of denial would be seeing inappropriate behavior and refusing to believe what you see. This can lead a principal to downplay inappropriate behavior by trying to make it appear that it is not as great a problem as it really is. This tendency is seen in the following comments made by a principal upon receiving a complaint about a teacher: "Yes, he seems to be a little too affectionate with students, but that is just his style; he does not mean anything by it." This rationalization allows the administrator to offer alibis, excuses, and justification for a colleague's inappropriate behavior. The first step in reducing the impact of bias is to evaluate all behaviors objectively. Consequently, a competent administrator must resist any inclination to discount data that points to a trusted colleague.

Conduct Training for All Staff

Failing to conduct appropriate training for secretaries, bus drivers, cafeteria staff, custodians, and all other support staff creates a significant information gap. All staff must know the behaviors that are prohibited and that they are responsible for reporting suspected abuse.

Enforce the Anti-Fraternization Policy

Colleagues of educators who have been convicted of sexually exploiting students frequently comment that in retrospect, they remember behavior that seemed "odd," or made them feel uncomfortable. In some cases it was common knowledge that students met frequently at educators' houses for parties or to watch movies. In one case a student was frequently excused from class to go to a teacher's room for non-instructional purposes. In other cases, educators gave students flowers, sent them cards, and bought them expensive gifts. In one case a teacher locked the classroom door and pulled down the window shades when he was meeting with students. In another case a teacher was seen eating breakfast at an out-of-town hotel with one of his students. Educators should not engage in sexual teasing or frequent or prolonged hugging, nor should they tell sexual jokes, or touch a student's hair or body. (See Appendix B for an example of an anti-fraternization policy.)

Keep Up-to-Date on Current Legal Issues

A professional is a person who is well trained. However, being a professional means more than simply acquiring a degree. A professional must continue to learn and practice his or her profession in a way that reflects current research and is in accordance with contemporary legal interpretations. The law plays a much greater role in educational administration than it did even a decade ago. Consequently, every educational leader should (a) be an active member of at least one professional association, (b) subscribe to and read at least one publication that focuses on school legal issues, and (c) annually attend at least one national or regional conference that focuses on legal issues.

Educate Parents About Exploitation

In order for the school to protect students from educator sexual exploitation, it must have a partnership with parents. The principal should encourage parents to talk with their youngsters about what happens in school. These conversations should go beyond the nonconversation, "How was school today?" "Fine." Parents must take any complaint of exploitation seriously. They must be encouraged to report any behavior that makes their child uncomfortable. Education and communication are the best lines of defense against child exploitation. Parents should be encouraged to supervise their children's Internet activities (i.e., chat groups, instant messages, Web site visits, e-mail).

The principal should provide each parent with a copy of the school's sexual exploitation prevention policy. Parents should be asked to show their support for the rules and help their child understand the reasons for them. Parents should be warned not to confront the alleged exploiter directly. In addition to the danger of violence, a confrontation will warn the accused and any subsequent investigation may be compromised. Warning also may result in intimidation of or retaliation against the child.

Educate Students About Exploitation

Students must understand the concept of appropriate boundaries. Students should not be expected to take total responsibility for reporting sexual exploitation. However, they should know and understand the school's code of conduct, and they should be taught to model responsible behavior. They should tell any educator or student who touches them in an inappropriate manner to stop, and then report the incident to a responsible adult. If inappropriate behavior persists, they should report the behavior to the school principal. They should keep any sexually harassing letters or e-mails that they receive, and also share this material with a parent, guardian, or other adult. Students should be encouraged to listen to their friends and pay attention to what is going on in their lives. If a friend shares information about a secret or special relationship she has with an educator, the student should encourage her friend to tell a trusted adult, such as a parent, a school psychologist, or the school principal. If the exploited student does not tell, the student's friend should tell someone.

Miscellaneous Information

Keep the superintendent informed of any potential problem before it becomes a crisis. Keep a log of each critical incident that takes place on campus. Keep a log of all appointments with parents, staff, and students. Generally, these logs should be kept on file for at least three years. However, in cases involving allegations of sexual exploitation, these files should be retained indefinitely. Promptly investigate all complaints. Regular surveys should be conducted to monitor the school's climate regarding sexual exploitation.

ACTION STEPS FOR EDUCATORS

Heighten Awareness of Sexual Exploitation

Even the appearance of impropriety may significantly damage an educator's reputation. The best way for educators to protect themselves from false accusations is to avoid behaviors that could be misconstrued.

- Do not remain alone with a student in the classroom outside of the regular school day without informing the principal.
- Do not remain alone with a student behind a closed door. (If the classroom door does not have a window, one should be installed.)
- Do not make a habit of meeting students outside of school for a meal, a soft drink, or a cup of coffee.
- Do not counsel students in nonacademic matters. (If an educator believes a student is in some type of trouble, the student should be referred to the "student at risk" team.)
- Do not regularly transport students in your own vehicle or allow students to have access to your vehicle.
- Do not engage students in conversations regarding their romantic or sexual activities.
- Do not entertain students in your home unless it is a school-sponsored activity.
- Do not make sexual comments, make comments about the students' bodies, tell sexual jokes, or share sexually oriented material with students.
- Do not touch students in a manner that a reasonable person could interpret as inappropriate.

POSTSCRIPT

Victims of sexual exploitation change their attitudes about school and themselves. Imagine what it must be like for children to know that when they come to school, they will be threatened, degraded, and exploited by an educator. Victims of sexual exploitation may develop a sense of helplessness and lowered self-esteem. Students often attempt to escape the exploitation by planning activities in a way that allows them to avoid certain students or educators. Their inability to find protection from sexual exploitation often results in anger, fear, and shame. When complaints are not taken seriously and responded to promptly, students rightly feel that they have been betrayed. Targets of sexual exploitation can be profoundly stigmatized and become isolated and withdrawn from others.

All competent educators are committed to eradicating sexual exploitation from their schools. These educators work in school districts that have developed comprehensive school-board-approved policies and conducted training sessions for students and all of their employees. These districts understand that staff development is only the first step in preventing sexual exploitation. Consequently, they are developing educational programs that ensure that each student knows the causes and consequences of sexual exploitation, and knows what to do if he or she believes a behavior is inappropriate. Even if a school district has a written policy and trains all school employees, unless it trains its students, it is unlikely that they will know how to respond to exploitation. Educators should not be solely responsible for eradicating sexual exploitation. Each member of the school community, including parents and students, must share in the responsibility. The first generation of training focused on how to recognize sexual exploitation when it occurred and what to do after it occurred. The current generation of training involves students and parents in creating a school climate that will not tolerate sexual exploitation. Although it is very important to stop existing sexual exploitation, it is also critical to prevent it before it starts.

It is encouraging to see that an increasing number of school districts are integrating information about sexual exploitation into their curricula. These programs focus on respecting oneself and respecting others. Many of these programs educate students about assertiveness and focus on resisting peer pressure and eliminating sexual stereotyping. These training sessions explain what sexual exploitation is, why it is prohibited, and what students should do if they become uncomfortable.

Appendix A

Steps to Follow in Developing a Sexual Exploitation Prevention Program

Sexual exploitation prevention programs will be more effective if parents and students are involved early in the process. It should be made clear that the school is not initiating the program because there is a problem. Rather, it is part of the school's safety program.

In order for a program of sexual exploitation prevention to be successful, it requires the attention of the superintendent and school board and the commitment of ample financial and human resources. The school board must make a public affirmation that sexual exploitation is taken seriously and will not be tolerated. A public statement by the superintendent leaves no doubt that the leadership of the school district believes that sexual exploitation is wrong and they are working to eradicate it. The policy should be prominently displayed in the school, printed in the student and teacher handbooks, and distributed to all parents. All students, parents, educators, and support staff should attend training sessions at which the policy and the consequences of sexual exploitation are clearly explained.

Some school districts seem reluctant to take this step. Some believe that there is no problem in their district and they do not wish to "rile up the parents" unnecessarily. Others believe that there is nothing that can be done to prevent sexual exploitation. Still others fear that even discussing the topic will stimulate false complaints. If there is any doubt that the school district is serious about this topic, it is very likely that offenders will not modify their behavior and victims will not believe that the system will help them if they choose to complain. A comprehensive program will document that the district is behaving in a reasonable manner and consequently, the likelihood of liability is reduced.

The prevention program must include a clearly defined procedure for reporting alleged incidents of sexual exploitation. Specific individuals must be identified as responsible for receiving complaints and investigating allegations of sexual exploitation. (In the case of suspected sexual abuse the school must follow the state statute and report the abuse.) These individuals must be held accountable for the successful implementation of the program. Each school building should have a person designated to oversee any complaints of sexual exploitation. This person is usually the principal. At least one male and one female should be trained as investigators.

It is devastating evidence against a school district if it can be documented that the employees and students either did not know that a policy existed, or were unclear what steps they should take if they wished to complain about an alleged incident of sexual exploitation. School districts have lost lawsuits in cases where there was a policy in place, but it was not clearly understood or followed.

Responsibility

Although specific individuals should be held accountable for monitoring the educational climate, receiving reports of suspected sexual exploitation, and investigating complaints, preventing all forms of sexual exploitation is the responsibility of all employees. Since neither students nor employees can be under direct supervision at all times, they must learn to monitor themselves and their peers. All students should learn to recognize when something makes them uncomfortable. They should also know how to file a formal complaint. The school must empower its students and employees to know their rights. However, as they are gaining the knowledge and experience necessary to stand up for themselves, the school must actively protect them.

Training

School districts must have educational programs on sexual exploitation prevention for their students, parents, faculty, and staff. Some school districts adopt a policy and then do nothing to train members of the educational community. Much of the training that does exist consists of either a few minutes at the beginning of a general educator orientation meeting, or a one-time presentation by a local or visiting expert. This type of training does little more than frighten already paranoid educators. Even those districts that have a training program often fail to follow up on these introductory sessions. Little effort is made to inservice staff members who were absent at the training session. Many districts that conduct comprehensive training sessions train only educators and administrators. This presents a major problem. Many of the incidents of sexual exploitation involve charges against bus drivers, custodians, cooks, paraprofessionals, and parent volunteers. Members of these groups seldom receive any meaningful training.

The biggest mistake that districts make when it comes to training is in neglecting to make significant efforts to educate students about the causes and consequences of sexual exploitation. All students must receive age-appropriate and developmentally appropriate training. This training should be ongoing and structured to encourage appropriate behavior.

The training program should ensure that all employees (a) understand the difference between appropriate and inappropriate behavior, (b) can recognize specific examples of appropriate and inappropriate behavior, (c) understand their responsibilities under the state mandatory child abuse reporting laws, and (d) understand their responsibility to model compassionate, caring, respectful behaviors and to create a climate of emotional support.

The training program should ensure that all students (a) understand boundary issues, (b) understand that that no one has the right to touch them without their permission, (c) understand that no one has the right to harass, embarrass, intimidate, or abuse them, (d) understand that it is never appropriate for an educator to have a romantic relationship with a student, and (e) understand they are to report to the principal or their parents if anyone makes them feel uncomfortable in school.

These approaches alone will not guarantee that students will not be sexually exploited at school, but they will lay a positive foundation that will make it easier for students to seek help. This plan will also heighten everyone's scrutiny, and will help the school employees respond quickly and effectively when they suspect sexual exploitation.

The sexual exploitation prevention program is about respect. It discusses the dangers of sexual exploitation openly and creates ways for students to share their concerns. There should be no confusion about the need for educators to develop caring relationships with students. Without these relationships, it is unlikely that students will feel a sense of belonging, pride, and attachment to the school. No student wants to come to a place where his or her teachers do not establish important relationships. However, there are boundary issues that must be addressed. The program is based on the assumption that just as students need to master academic skills, they must also learn to interact appropriately with peers and adults.

As a result of a comprehensive sexual exploitation risk management program, a school climate develops that encourages staff members and students to raise concerns about observed early warning signs, and to immediately report all observations of imminent danger.

Appendix B

Model Sexual Exploitation Prevention Policy

1. All district employees, students, patrons, and vendors are entitled to work and study in school-related environments that are free from sexual exploitation. Therefore sexual exploitation or violence by any officer, employee, student, or other person having business with the district is prohibited. Sexual exploitation is any sexual advance, request for sexual favor, or sex-based behavior.

2. Any employee whose behavior is found to be in violation of this policy shall be subject to discipline, including but not limited to suspension or termination of employment.

3. All romantic relationships between students and employees are prohibited. Educators and students will not engage or attempt to engage in any nonprofessional social behavior with each other. Nonprofessional social behavior includes but is not limited to dating; any type of sexual activity; any touching of a sexual nature; hugging; kissing; hand holding or physical caressing; sexual flirtations, advances, or propositions; continued or repeated unwanted remarks about an individual's body; sexually degrading words used toward an individual or to describe an individual; the display in the school or workplace of sexually suggestive actions, gestures, objects, graffiti, or pictures.

4. A student who believes that he or she has suffered sexual exploitation should report such matter to the school principal.

5. The superintendent or designee shall assign an individual or team of individuals to investigate a complaint of sexual exploitation. A person who is alleged in a complaint to have violated this policy or to have been a witness to the alleged violation may not be named the investigator of the complaint.

6. If the allegation of sexual exploitation is made against the superintendent or a member of the board, the assistant superintendent for Human Resource Services shall appoint, with the board's legal counsel, an independent investigator not employed by the district. The superintendent or the board retains the prerogative to appoint an independent investigator for any allegation of sexual exploitation.

7. After completion of an investigation, if the investigator determines that sexual exploitation has taken place, disciplinary action will be taken.

8. Retaliation against a person who reports or testifies to a complaint of sexual exploitation is prohibited. Any retaliation shall itself be viewed as an instance of sexual harassment and be subject to the provisions of this policy.

9. To the extent reasonably possible, the privacy of a person involved in a sexual exploitation investigation shall be preserved. Investigators will request that participants in the investigation not discuss the investigation, except for conversations with parents, guardians, spouses, counselors, or legal representatives.

10. After an investigation has yielded a decision, either the person determined to have committed the exploitation or the person alleging the exploitation may appeal the decision to the superintendent, who will hear the appeal or designate a representative to hear the appeal.

11. If at any time during the investigation it is suspected that child abuse has occurred, a report shall be made to the state child protection agency.

Appendix C

Resources for Educators and Parents

American Humane Association, Children's Division (AHA)
63 Inverness Drive, East Englewood, CO 80112-5117
(800) 227-4645
info@americanhumane.org

American Professional Society on the Abuse of Children (APSAC)
PO Box 26901, CHO 3B-3406, Oklahoma City, OK 73190
(405) 271-8202
www.apsac.org

Center for Sex Offender Management (CSOM), Center for Effective
    Public Policy
8403 Colesville Road, Suite 720
Silver Spring, MD 20910
(301) 589-9383
askcsom@csom.org
www.csom.org

Center for the Prevention of Sexual and Domestic Violence (CPSDV)
2400 N. 45th Street, #10 Seattle, WA 98103
(206) 634-1903
cpsdv@cpsdv.org
www.cpsdv.org

Crimes Against Children Research Center (CCRC)
University of New Hampshire
20 College Road, #126
Horton Social Science Center, Durham, NH 03824
(603) 862-1888
www.unh.edu/ccrc/

Justice for Children (JFC)
2600 Southwest Freeway, Suite 806, Houston, TX 77098
(713) 225-4357
info@jsadvocacy.org

National Association of Child Advocates (NACA)
1522 K Street N.W., Suite 600
Washington, DC 20005-1202
(202) 289-0777
naca@childadvocacy.org

National Center for Assault Prevention (NCAP)
606 Delsea Drive, Sewell, NJ 08080-9199
(908) 369-8972
patstan@rcn.com
www.ncap.org

National Center for Missing and Exploited Children (NCMEC)
Charles B. Wang International Children Building
699 Prince Street Alexandria, VA 22314-3175
(703) 274-3900
www.ncmec.org

National Center for Victims of Crime (NCVC)
2000 M Street N.W., Suite 480, Washington, DC 20036
(800) 211-7996
webmaster@ncvc.org

National Child Abuse Hotline
15757 N. 78th Street, Scottsdale, AZ 85260
(480) 922-8212
www.childhelpusa.org

The National Children's Advocacy Center (NCAC)
200 Westside Square, Suite 700, Huntsville, AL 35801
(256) 533-0531
webmaster@ncac-hsv.org
www.ncac-hsv.org

National Children's Alliance (NCA)
1612 K Street N.W., Suite 500, Washington, DC 20006
(800) 239-9950
info@nca-online.org

National Clearinghouse on Child Abuse and Neglect (NCCAN)
300 C Street S.W., Washington, DC 20447
(800) 394-3366
nccanch@calib.com
www.calib.com/nccanch

The National Committee to Prevent Child Abuse
332 S. Michigan Ave., Suite 1600, Chicago, IL 60604
(800) 555-3748
www.childabuse.org/index.html

National Organization for Victim Assistance (NOVA)
1730 Park Road N.W., Washington, DC 20010
(202) 232-6682
nova@try-nova.org

The National Organization on Male Sexual Victimization (NOMSV)
PMB 103, 5505 Connecticut Ave. N.W., Washington, DC 20015-2601
(800) 738-4181
nomsv@nomsv.org

National Sexual Violence Resource Center (NSVRC)
123 North Enola Drive, Enola, PA 17025
(717) 909-0710
resources@nsvrc.org
www.nsvrc.org

Prevent Child Abuse America (PCAA)
200 South Michigan Ave., 17th Floor, Chicago, IL 60604-2404
(312) 663-3520
www.preventchildabuse.org

Rape, Abuse & Incest National Network (RAINN)
635-B Pennsylvania Ave. S.E., Washington, DC 20003
(800) 656-4673
rainnmail@aol.com
www.rainn.org

The Safer Society Foundation, Inc. (SSFI)
PO Box 340, Brandon, VT 05733-0340
(802) 247-3132
www.safersociety.org

Sex Abuse Treatment Alliance (SATA)
PO Box 1191, Okemos MI 48805-1191
(517) 482-2085
wayne@arq.net

STOP IT NOW!
PO Box 495, Haydenville, MA 01039
(413) 268-3096
info@stopitnow.org
www.stopitnow.org

Appendix D

Sexual Harassment and Exploitation Prevention Assessment

To score this assessment, check each item that your school has in place. Add one point for each item you have checked. Total your points and use the scale at the end of the assessment to evaluate your district's sexual harassment and exploitation prevention quotient (SEPA).

1. _____ A sexual harassment and exploitation prevention policy has been adopted by the school board.

2. _____ All administrators of the school district are thoroughly familiar with the policy.

3. _____ A copy of the policy is included in the faculty handbook.

4. _____ All certified staff members have been trained to recognize and prevent sexual harassment and exploitation.

5. _____ All certified staff members know their responsibilities under this policy.

6. _____ All classified staff members have been trained to recognize and prevent sexual harassment and sexual exploitation.

7. _____ There is a grievance procedure included in the policy.

8. _____ Investigators have been identified and trained in the investigation protocol.

9. _____ The student handbook for secondary school students includes a comprehensive treatment of sexual harassment and exploitation prevention.

10. _____ The student handbook for elementary school students includes an age-appropriate treatment of sexual harassment and exploitation prevention.

11. ____ All secondary school students have been trained in sexual harassment and exploitation prevention and understand what to do in the face of harassing or exploitative behavior.

12. ____ All elementary school students have been trained in sexual harassment and exploitation prevention and understand what to do in the face of exploitative behavior.

13. ____ There is a procedure in place to ensure that all new employees are informed about the sexual harassment and exploitation policy.

14. ____ All off-campus sites are informed about the school district's sexual harassment and exploitation prevention policy and informed that it covers all school-sponsored activities.

15. ____ Information about sexual harassment and exploitation has been integrated across the curriculum.

16. ____ All parents have received a copy of the sexual harassment and exploitation prevention policy and have been informed that the school does not tolerate sexual harassment or exploitation.

17. ____ The district's sexual harassment and exploitation prevention policy and its educational efforts are regularly featured in the school district's newsletters.

18. ____ Regular surveys of students and staff are conducted to monitor the school's climate regarding sexual harassment and exploitation.

19. ____ There is a plan in place to regularly evaluate the policy and educational program.

20. ____ Every allegation of sexual harassment or sexual exploitation is taken seriously and investigated promptly.

Scale

16–20 points: Your school district has obviously made a significant, concerted effort to develop and implement a comprehensive program of sexual harassment and sexual exploitation prevention.

11–15 points: Although your district has made some effort at preventing sexual harassment and exploitation, much additional effort is needed.

0–10 points: Your district does not appear to have made a commitment to preventing and eradicating sexual harassment and exploitation. In order to protect your students from sexual harassment and exploitation, and your school district from legal liability, you need to address these deficiencies.

Glossary

acquaintance rape.   Unwanted sexual intercourse, oral sex, anal sex, or other sexual contact with the use of force or threat of force by someone known by the victim.

boundaries.   Internally or externally imposed limits that define appropriate relationships between individuals.

child molestation.   The crime of sexual acts with children under the age of 18, including touching of private parts, exposure of genitalia, taking of pornographic pictures, rape, and inducement to sexual acts with the molester or with other children.

coercive exploitation.   Exploitation in which the abuser either threatens to withhold something the youngster desires, or promises to reward the youngster with a benefit or privilege.

defamation.   A false claim, published to a third party, that injures a person's good name or reputation.

delayed discovery doctrine.   A doctrine that holds that the limitation period does not begin to run until the plaintiff has discovered, or in the exercise of reasonable diligence should have discovered, all of the facts which are essential to the cause of action.

discriminatory enforcement.   Enforcement in which the severity of the punishment that a child molester receives depends on his or her sex or sexual orientation.

exclusive type pedophile.   A pedophile who is sexually attracted only to children.

fraternization.   Acts of sexual intimacy, or other physical touching of a romantic or sexual nature, or public displays of affection between students and staff members of the same or opposite sex.

hostile environment sexual harassment.   Sexual harassment that is characterized by multiple, varied, and frequent occurrences, and is sufficiently severe, persistent, or pervasive to limit a student's ability to participate in or benefit from the education program.

in loco parentis.   The concept that the school stands in the place of the parent.

intimate exploitation.   Exploitation in which the exploiter leads the youngster to believe he or she has a genuine desire for a mutually committed intimate relationship.

liberty interest.   An individual's right to engage in an occupation, among other things.

Megan's Law.   A federal law that requires sex offender registration and community notification. It allows the states discretion to establish criteria for disclosure, but compels them to make information on registered sex offenders available to the public.

mobile molester.   An educator who molests children in one district and then is allowed to resign and continue molesting in other districts. Also known as "passing the trash."

negligence.   The omission to do something a reasonable person would do, or the doing of something that a reasonable person would not do.

nonexclusive type pedophile.   A pedophile who is sexually attracted to both children and adults.

pedophile.   An individual who is sexually attracted to prepubescent children, and who is aged 16 years or older and at least 5 years older than the child.

pedophilia.   A psychological disorder that involves sexual activity with a prepubescent child (generally aged 13 years or younger).

preferential child molester.   A child molester who is a pedophile and usually maintains this desire throughout his or her life.

property interest.   Educators gain property interest in their employment when they receive tenure or a continuing contract.

qualified immunity doctrine.   The doctrine that grants government officials immunity from civil liability so long as their conduct does not violate clearly established statutory or constitutional rights.

quid pro quo sexual harassment.   Sexual demands made upon a student in exchange for educational participation, advancement, or other benefits, or made under the threat of punishment.

recidivism.   The tendency to return to criminal activities and behaviors.

recovered memories.   Memories of an abusive incident that are recalled many years after the abuse.

respondeat superior.   The doctrine that an employer is liable for the actions of employees in the course of employment.

sexual abuse.   Criminal sexual conduct that involves physical contact between the abuser and victim, and a significant age difference between the parties.

sexual assault.   Any genital, oral, or anal penetration by a part of the accused's body or by an object, using force or without the victim's consent.

sexual coercion.   Unwanted sexual intercourse, or any other sexual contact, subsequent to the use of menacing verbal pressure or misuse of authority.

sexual harassment.   Unwelcome contact of a sexual nature that interferes with a school employee's ability to do his or her job or with a student's ability to enjoy the benefits of an education.

sexual molestation.   The crime of sexual acts with children under the age of 18.

situational child molester. A child molester who does not possess a genuine sexual preference for children, but will molest a child because he has access to the child.

statute of limitation.   A statute that prescribes limits to the rights of a person to bring a civil suit, or a government to initiate criminal prosecution.

Type I abuse.   Sexual abuse involving a survivor who was always aware of the abuse, but was unaware of the connection between the abuse and his or her physical or psychological symptoms.

Type II abuse.   Sexual abuse involving survivors who repress all memory of the abuse.

unwelcome.   Attention that is not requested or invited and is regarded as undesirable or offensive.

vicarious liability.   Liability for the negligent actions of another person.

References

AdvocateWeb. (n.d.). Retrieved September 27, 2002, from www.advocateweb.org

American Association of University Women. (2001). *Hostile hallways: Bullying, teasing, and sexual harassment in school.* Washington, DC: Author.

American Psychiatric Association. (1994). *Diagnostic and statistical manual of mental disorders* (4th ed.). Washington, DC: Author.

Answers to commonly asked questions about child sexual abuse. (n.d.). Retrieved December 1, 2002, from www.stopitnow.com/comquest.html

Arizona Department of Education. (2003, April 22). Superintendent Tom Horne announces important guidelines on reporting child abuse and professional misconduct [Press Release].

Bethel Sch. Dist. No. 403 v. Fraser ex rel. Fraser, 478 U.S. 675 (1986).

Black's Law Dictionary (7th ed.). (1999). St. Paul, MN: West Publishing.

Boodman, S. G. (2002, July 29). How deep the scars of abuse? Some victims crippled; others stay resilient [Electronic version]. *Washington Post*, p. A1.

Browne, A., & Finkelhor, D. (1986). *Impact of child sexual abuse: A review of the research.* Ottawa: Minister of Supply and Services. (Reprinted from *Psychological Bulletin, 99*, 66–77)

Campbell v. Robinson, 955 S.W.2d 609 (Tenn. Ct. App. 1997).

Center for the Prevention of School Violence. (2000). *A vision for safe schools.* Raleigh, NC: Author.

Child Abuse and Neglect Prevention and Treatment Act, 42 U.S.C.A. § 5106 (West Supp. 2001).

Chronis, P. (2002, May 22). Pacelli assistant football coach charged with sex assault of child. *Stevens Point Journal*, pp. A1, A5.

Civil Action for Deprivation of Rights Act, 42 U.S.C. § 1983 (1994).

Community Protection Act, Wash. Rev. Code Ann. § 4.24.550 (2002).

Conn. Dep't of Public Safety v. Doe, 122 S. Ct. 1959 (2002).

Conn. Dep't of Public Safety v. Doe, 123 S. Ct. 1160 (2003).

Crosson-Tower, C. (2002). *When children are abused: An educator's guide to intervention.* Boston: Allyn & Bacon.

Davis v. Monroe County Bd. of Educ., 526 U.S. 629 (1999).

DeMitchell, T. A. (2002). The duty to protect: Blackstone's doctrine of in loco parentis: A lens for viewing the sexual abuse of students. *Brigham Young University Education & Law Journal* [Online], *17*. 17700 words. Available: Lexis-Nexis Academic Universe [2002, May 24].

DeRose v. Carswell, 242 Cal. Rptr. 368 (1987).

DiCosala v. Kay, 450 A.2d 508 (1982).

Drummond, S., & Hendrie, C. (1998, December 2, 9, 16). A trust betrayed: Sexual abuse by teachers. *Education Week.*

Dunn, A. (2001). Statutes of limitation on sexual assault crimes: Has the availability of DNA evidence rendered them obsolete? *University of Arkansas at Little Rock Law Review* [Online], *23.* 15186 words. Available: Lexis-Nexis Academic Universe [2002, April 20].

Dwyer, K., & Osher, D. (2000). *Safeguarding our children: An action guide.* Washington, DC: U.S. Departments of Education and Justice, American Institutes for Research.

Dwyer, K., Osher, D., & Warger, C. (1998). *Early warning, timely answer: A guide to safe schools.* Washington, DC: U.S. Department of Education.

Ehrlich, S. C. (1997). The investigation process. In B. Sandler & R. Shoop (Eds.), *Sexual Harassment on Campus* (pp. 163-185). Boston: Allyn and Bacon.

Facts about those abused and those who abuse. (n.d.). Retrieved October 23, 2002, from www.stopitnow.com/csafacts.html

False Memory Syndrome Foundation. (n.d.). *Memory and Reality.* Retrieved December 12, 2002, from www.fmsfonline.org

Farmer, T. (2001, August 15). Victims confront molester Reardon: "You ruined my life." *Boston Herald*, pp. A1, A24.

Fine, L. (2000, November 8). Jury awards $105 million in teacher-student abuse case. *Education Week.* Retrieved May 1, 2002, from www.edweek.org

Finkelhor, D. (1994). Current information on the scope and nature of child sexual abuse. *The Future of Children: Sexual Abuse of Children, 4*(2), 31–51.

Franklin v. Gwinnett County Public Schools, 503 U.S. 60 (1992).

Frawley-O'Dea, M. (2002). *The experience of the victim of sexual abuse: A reflection.* Retrieved August, 2002, from www.usccb.org/bishops/frawley.htm

Friedman, J., & Boumil, M. M. (1995). *Betrayal of trust: Sex and power in professional relationships.* Westport, CT: Praeger.

Garcia v. City of N.Y., 646 N.Y.S.2d 508, 509 (App. Div. 1st Dep't 1996).

Gebser v. Lago Vista Independent School District, 524 U.S. 274 (1998).

Gilot, L. (2002, July 11). Longtime area coach accused of molesting. *El Paso Times*, p. 3.

Goldberg, B. (Writer), & Winn, J. (Director). (2001). Passing the trash [Television series episode]. In A. Martin (Producer), *Real Sports With Bryant Gumbel.* New York: HBO.

Goldin v. Board of Educ. of Cent. School Dist. No. 1, Towns of Brookhaven & Smithtown, 45 A.D.2d 870 (1974).

Groth, A. N. (1982). The incest offender. In S. Sgroi (Ed.), *Handbook of clinical intervention in child sexual abuse.* Lexington, MA: Lexington Books.

Groth, A. N., & Birnbaum, H. J. (1978). Adult sexual orientation and attraction to underage persons. *Archives of Sexual Behavior, 7*(3), 175–181.

Guidelines on Discrimination Because of Sex, 29 C.F.R. § 1604.11 (1992).

Hanson, R. K. (1996). *Child molester recidivism.* Retrieved May 1, 2002, from Solicitor General Canada Web site: www.sgc.gc.ca/publications/corrections/199670_e.asp

Hanson, R. K. (1997). *Predictors of sex offense recidivism.* Retrieved September 1, 2002, from Solicitor General Canada Web site: www.sgc.gc.ca/publications/corrections/199779_e.asp

Hanson, R. K., & Bussiere, M. T. (1996). *Predictors of sexual offender recidivism: A meta-analysis* (Cat. No. JS4-1/1996–4E). Ottawa: Solicitor General Canada.

Heline, M. G. (2002, May 16). Misdemeanor for Woods: Felony would burden ex-coach's children. *South Bend Tribune*, pp. A1, A6.

Hendrie, C. (1998). Sex with students: When employees cross the line. *Education Week, 18*(14), 1, 12–14.

Hendrie, C. (2003, April 30). States target sexual abuse by educators. *Education Week.* Retrieved April 30, 2003, from www.edweek.org

Holmes, W. C., & Slap, G. B. (1998). Sexual abuse of boys: Definition, prevalence, correlates, sequelae, and management. *Journal of the American Medical Association, 280*, 1855–1862.

Hopper, J. (2002). *Sexual abuse of males: Prevalence, possible lasting effects, and resources.* Retrieved August 4, 2002, from www.jimhopper.com

How to investigate reports of employee sexual misconduct. (2002, April). *Private School Director's Legal Guide*, 1–4.

Jacob Wetterling Crimes Against Children and Sexually Violent Offender Registration Act, 42 U.S.C. § 14071 (1994).

Jenny, C., & Roesler, T. A. (1994). Are children at risk for sexual abuse by homosexuals? *Pediatrics, 94*(1), 41–44.

Jerry v. Board of Education, 324 N.E.2d 106 (1974).

John R. v. Oakland Unified School District, 48 Cal. 3d 438 (March 30, 1989).

Johnson, G. (2002, May 20). School district, police cleared in Fualaau case. *Seattle Post-Intelligencer.* Retrieved May 21, 2002, from seattlepi.nwsource.com/local/71182_fualaau20ww.shtml

Johnson v. Johnson, 701 F. Supp. 1363 (E.D. Ill. 1988).

Kalichman, S. C. (1993). *Mandated reporting of suspected child abuse: Ethics, law, and policy.* Washington, DC: American Psychological Association.

Latimer, J. (1998). *The consequences of child maltreatment: A reference guide for health practitioners.* Retrieved April 23, 2003, from Health Canada Web site: www.hc-sc.gc.ca/hppb/familyviolence/html/98p057e0.html

LeBlanc, C. (2002). *Coach guilty of sexual assaults.* Retrieved November 10, 2002, from www.thestate.com

Lienhard, R. (1996). Negligent retention of employees: An expanding doctrine. *Defense Counsel Journal, 63*, 389.

Lyle v. Hancock Place Sch. Dist. No. 19, 1716 P.2d 724 (Or. 1986).

Markovitz, B. (2000, June). Public school teachers as plaintiffs in defamation suits: Do they deserve actual malice? *Georgetown Law Journal* [Online], *88*, 20509 words. Available: Lexis-Nexis Academic Universe [2002, November].

Megan's Law, Pub. L. No. 104-145, 110 Stat. 1345 (1996).

Munro, K. (2000). *Incest and child sexual abuse: Definitions, perpetrators, victims, and effects.* Retrieved December 12, 2002, from www.kalimunro.com/article_sexualabuse.html

Nack, W., & Yaeger, D. (1999, September 13). Every parent's nightmare. *Sports Illustrated, 91*(10), 40–51.

National Alliance for Youth Sports. (n.d.). Retrieved December 20, 2002, from www.nays.org

National Clearinghouse on Child Abuse and Neglect Information. (2002). Retrieved November 1, 2002, from www.calib.com/nccanch/

National Research Council. (1993). *Understanding child abuse and neglect.* Washington, DC: National Academy Press.

No harm, no worry, no jail in teacher-pupil sex case. (2002, May 24). Retrieved April 22, 2003, from www.warrencoea.org

Oberman, M. (2000). Regulating consensual sex with minors: Defining a role for statutory rape. *Buffalo Law Review* [Online], *48.* 33440 words. Available: Lexis-Nexis Academic Universe [2003, March].

Otte v. Doe, 534 U.S. 1126 (2002).

Peterson, M. R. (1992). *At personal risk: Boundary violations in professional relationships.* New York: W. W. Norton.

Pochna, P. (2002). Women as sex offenders on the rise. *North Jersey News.* Retrieved December 1, 2002, from www.bergen.com

Pryor, D. W. (1996). *Unspeakable acts: Why men sexually abuse children.* New York: New York University Press.

Puit, G. (2002, May 7). Police affidavit says teacher had sex with teen. *Las Vegas Review-Journal,* pp. 1B, 7B.

Randi W. v. Murdoc Joint Unified School District, 929 P.2d 582 (1997).

Restatement (Second) of Torts § 596 (1977).

Reynolds, L. A. (1997). *People with mental retardation & sexual abuse.* Retrieved November 11, 2002, from www.advocateweb.org

Richmond Newspapers, Inc. v. Lipscomb, 362 S.E.2d 32 (Va. 1987).

Ross, V. J., & Marlowe, J. (1985). *The forbidden apple: Sex in the schools.* Palm Springs, CA: ETC Publications.

Sansom, P., & Kemerer, F. (2002). It's all about rules. *Education Law Reports, 166,* 395–414.

Santschi, D. (2002, May 26). Abuse at schools holds aftermath. *Riverside Press-Enterprise,* pp. B01, B04.

Schubert, M. (2002, May 29). Allegations truthful, ex-student maintains. *Pasadena Star-News.* Retrieved June 6, 2002, from www.pasadenastarnews.com

Scott County School Dist. No. 2 v. Dietrich, 499 N.E.2d 11710 (Ind. App. 1986).

SESAME (Stop Educator Sexual Abuse, Misconduct & Exploitation). Retrieved September 13, 2002, from www.sesamenet.org

Sexual Harassment Guidance: Harassment of Students by School Employees, Other Students, or Third Parties, 62 Fed. Reg. §§ 12034, 12037 (Mar. 13, 1997).

Sexual harassment: It's hurting people [Video]. (1994). Overland Park, KS: Quality Work Environments.

Shakeshaft, C., & Cohan, A. (1995, March). Sexual abuse of students by school personnel. *Phi Delta Kappan, 76,* 512–520.

Shoop, R. J. (1999, May/June). Sexual abuse of students by teachers. *The High School Magazine, 6*(7), 9–12.

Shoop, R. J. (2000, September). The principal's dilemma: Protecting students from abuse while protecting a teacher's reputation. *Principal Leadership,* 22–27.

Shoop, R. J. (2002, March). Identifying a standard of care. *Principal Leadership,* 48–52.

Shoop, R. J., & Dunklee, D. R. (2001, April). The hazardous waters of staff selection. *Principal Leadership,* 9–13.

Shoop, R. J., & Dunklee, D. R. (2002, December). Risk management. *Principal Leadership,* 28–32.

Shoop, R. J., & Hayhow, J. (1994). *Sexual harassment in our schools: What teachers and parents need to know to spot it and stop it.* Boston: Allyn & Bacon.

Simpson, M. (2002, September 28). Teacher to be tried for teen affair in 1978–79. *San Diego Union-Tribune.* Retrieved October 1, 2002, from www.signonsandiego. com/news/northcounty/

Sobsey, D. (1994). *Violence and abuse in the lives of people with disabilities: The end of silent acceptance?* Baltimore: Paul H. Brookes.

Stevenson, M. R. (2000). Public policy, homosexuality, and the sexual coercion of children. *Journal of Psychology & Human Sexuality, 12*(4), 1–19.

Teacher jailed for sex with student. (2002, May 24). *The Columbus Ledger-Enquirer.* Retrieved September 6, 2002, from www.ledgerenquirer.com

Title IX of the Education Amendments of 1972, 20 U.S.C. § 1681(a) (1972).

Turner v. South-Western City Sch. Dist., 82 F. Supp. 2d 757 (S.D. Ohio 1999).

Tyson v. Tyson, 727 P.2d 226, 227 (Wash. 1986).

U.S. Advisory Board on Child Abuse and Neglect. (1990). *Child abuse and neglect: Critical first steps in answer to a national emergency.* Washington, DC: U.S. Department of Health and Human Services.

U.S. Department of Education, Office for Civil Rights. (2001, January). *Revised sexual harassment guidance: Harassment of students by school employees, other students, or third parties.* Retrieved March 1, 2002, from www.ed.gov/offices/OCR/shguide/index.html

Valenti-Hein, D., & Schwartz, L. (1995). *The sexual abuse interview for those with developmental disabilities.* Santa Barbara, CA: James Stanfield.

Woman suing school over coach's sex history. (2002, September 22). *News & Observer of Raleigh, North Carolina.* Retrieved September 22, 2002, from www. newsobserver.com

Wood v. Strickland, 420 U.S. 308 (1975).

Index

CORWIN
PRESS

The Corwin Press logo—a raven striding across an open book—represents the union of courage and learning. Corwin Press is committed to improving education for all learners by publishing books and other professional development resources for those serving the field of K–12 education. By providing practical, hands-on materials, Corwin Press continues to carry out the promise of its motto: **"Helping Educators Do Their Work Better."**